# BEHIND THE WOODEN Counter

## PEARL HUTCHINSON

BT57    BYY

# DEDICATION:

To the memory of my much loved parents Charles and Jean Kee
and to my Uncle Jimmy who was a great storyteller.

Published 2014
© Pearl Hutchinson

ISBN: 978-1-906689-56-8

Printed by Impact Printing, Coleraine & Ballycastle

# INTRODUCTION

In rural Ireland the country shop, together with the church and the school, was an integral part of Irish life.

The shop was usually attached to a dwelling house for the shopkeeper and his family. Many could be found at the crossroads where, traditionally, country folk would gather.

It was a place for people to meet, to talk and to laugh. At times it was a place to share secrets or unburden a grief.

The shopkeeper was someone who knew about their situation and could be relied upon in difficult times when money was scarce.

Customers were all country folk. Their families, having lived in the same place for generations, knew a lot about each other. The traditional home was either a large two-storied house or a thatched cottage with whitewashed walls and a half door. Until the 1960's, the old way of life continued. Modern conveniences took some time to come. Transport was limited, with few people owning cars, so local shops were essential.

For 50 years the country shop has been in decline. Where once there were shops every couple of miles. Today, it is rare to find any.

Large supermarkets now dominate almost every town. Bulk buying means that prices are kept lower and small shops can not compete. The conveyor belt at the tills means that customers must keep on the move.

The personal touch and interest in the customer's life is gone.

# iv
# CONTENTS

# MY FATHER'S COUNTRY SHOP

My father's shop was situated in the Finn Valley in Co. Donegal. It was five miles from the twin towns of Ballybofey and Stranorlar.

Our parish was divided by the River Finn. By the time the river reached us it had widened and deepened. It was not only our playground but a paradise for anglers from many parts of Ireland and further afield.

From our veranda window we could see both up and down the road. To the west was Altnapaste, rising 1199ft above sea level. When the mist came down the mountain we did not need a forecast to tell us the rain was coming.

Down the road, John's Brae was clearly visible. Beyond was St. John's Church. It stood among the trees beside the river.

*St. John's Church Kilteevogue*

The main road to Glenties passed over the bridge towards Welchtown.

A Welsh family by the name of Davis had complied with the terms of the Plantation of Ulster and built "a bawn of stone and clay, rough cast with lime, having two flanking towers and a stone house on it."
The Davises planted the place with 32 families of Welsh extraction and were capable of supplying the King with 54 men-at-arms.
It is interesting to note that my father was asked on many occasions in later life if he was Welsh. His accent had the remnants of a Welsh lilt.

One of the Davis family became Lord Mountcashell on marrying a MacCarthy of Cork. He was the landowner who drew up an indenture with the Kee brothers in 1733 for the townland of Meenagrave in the parish of Kilteevogue.

It is where our shop was situated.

Wooden counters ran right round the shop. Two large windows brought light to the interior. In earlier times oil lamps hung from the ceiling and brass scales sat on the counter.

The shop was divided into two sections - grocery and hardware. All the goods were displayed behind the counter. Shelving to the ceiling was needed for the many items for sale. There were cupboards for bread and small drawers for spices and snuff. There were bins for tea and sugar and a glass case for medicines.

In the hardware section there were items that are now found in antique shops. Blue and white bowls, half sets of china, dipped pens and every other item needed by the housewife in a rural community.

There was an unwritten rule that customers were not allowed behind the counter. It was the shopkeeper's territory. He was there to serve.

Thomas Kee, my father's uncle, built the shop.

As two of his brothers were on the family farm he had to look in another direction for work. A position of shop boy became available in a shop a few hundred yards from his home. Tom went to McCreery's to learn his trade. They had a thriving business. However, his ambition was to have a shop of his own. He planned it to the finest detail.

His brother Charles carted the stones from the hill on the farm.
About 1890 Tom started his own business. For a number of years the shop was run from the sitting room in the house.

"Paradise House" was the name that he gave his new home. It was his dream fulfilled.

*Paradise House and shop as viewed from The Orchard*

**4**

*This memo page was found among my father's papers*

MEMO.

RAIL—GLENMORE.

Meenagrave, Welchtown, ————————————— 194

Co. Donegal.

Thomas Kee,

GENERAL GROCER.

HARDWARE. :: CHINA & GLASS STORE.

The customers came from a wide area. In Tom's day, the usual mode of transport was by foot. Two shop boys were needed when trade was booming. In 1911 John George Kee and Charles Fooks were employed. Both were 18 years old. Old ladies in black shawls, came with their baskets tucked under their arms. They would stop occasionally for a rest or greet a neighbour passing on the road. Sometimes they would get a lift on a horse and trap, or a cart. Most preferred to walk.

In the shop there was a bench where they could rest their weary legs. Young and old liked to sit there while they were being served. There were those customers who loved a bit of fun and would start an argument. If a row broke out Tom would chase the offenders up the road with a shovel!

*Tom and Lizzie Kee*

In 1895 Tom brought his young bride, Elizabeth Stevenson, to Paradise House.

Cloghan Station, Ballybofey.

# TRANSPORTATION OF GOODS

In those early years the goods were transported by the railway to Glenmore station. When a branch line of the wee Donegal, as it was known, opened to Glenties from Stranorlar in 1895 it proved to be an important link in getting goods to the shop. In earlier times the goods had to be transported from Stranorlar station by Tom's brothers with their horse and cart. If the family was out working in the fields everything was dropped if Tom needed to get the goods from the station.

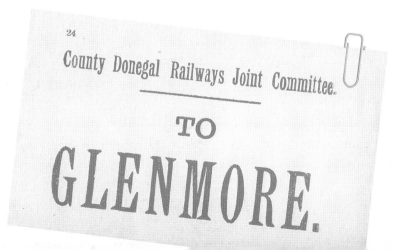

24

County Donegal Railways Joint Committee.

TO

GLENMORE.

C.D.R.J.C.

This ticket is issued subject to
the Printed Bye-Laws, Regulations
& Notices of the Committee.

Third Class          Fare 2s. 2d.

(A)          Glenmore
               TO
          GLENTIES

0021

*Cloghan Station, Co. Donegal*

*Out in the fields cutting the corn*

Young Jimmy felt it a great honour when he was sent to the station in Glenmore with Bessie the mare. Sometimes there would be 3 tons of flour or feeding stuff to transport. It was hard work carrying an 8st bag of flour up the stairs and into the loft. However, he was always rewarded with a bag of sweets. His father got a ½ oz of tobacco and his mother got flour for baking.

*Charles and Elizabeth Kee outside "The Orchard"*
*with five of their children*

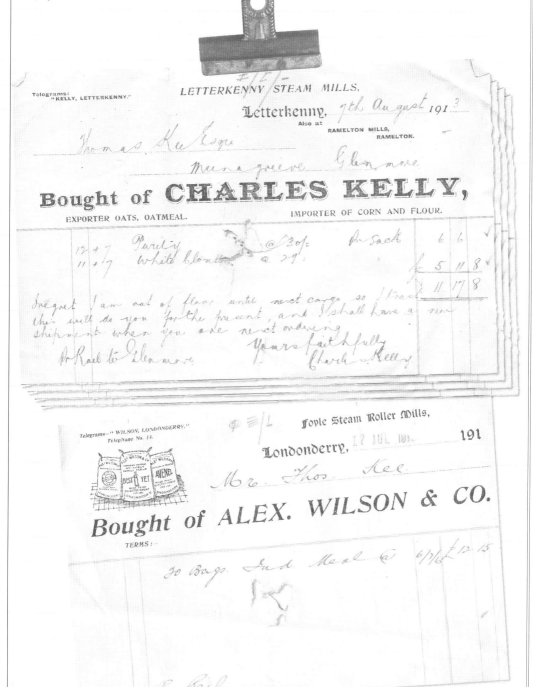

Two interesting old bill heads were found, dated 1913.

*Charles Kelly writes on his invoice that he is out of flour until the next cargo.*

Eggs were bought in large quantities and packed in straw. They were transported by horse and cart at 6 o'clock in the morning to the station for the first train. They were bound for Scotland.

*This old postcard gives an idea on how the eggs were packed*

## Prices for 1916-1917

| | |
|---|---|
| 1lb. tea | 2s.8d |
| 1lb. ham | 1s 4d |
| ½ lb. cheese | 7d |
| ½ lb. biscuits | 4½d |
| Laces | 2d |
| 2 bars of soap | 6d. |
| ½ st. sugar | 2s. 11d |
| 2lb. onions | 6d |
| 1 lb rice | 4d |
| 1 lb. barley | 5d |

To supplement their income many housewives sold home-made butter to the shop. In 1917 the price fluctuated from 1s 8d to 2s. per pound.
This helped to reduce the shopping bill.

The new century brought many changes. Tenant farmers were at last able to own their own land but it was still a struggle to survive. The only jobs available for young people were at the Hiring fairs. Strabane was the biggest in the area. Conditions were often harsh for those who were hired but the money was eagerly awaited at the end of the 6 months. It was handed over when the person returned home, where it was badly needed.

It was difficult for many customers to pay their bills in the shop. Tom was known to be lenient to his customers who had fallen on hard times. He was prepared to wait, which was sometimes a long time.

Civil war brought unrest in Ireland. Rumours abounded in the shop about raids on farms looking for arms. Next came the First World War with many casualties among the young men from the district who enlisted.

Through all the tough times, Tom worked hard to build up a thriving business. His ledgers were neatly written in a copperplate hand. He could afford some luxuries to enhance his life.

The dwelling house was filled with fine furniture. Tom and Lizzie liked to entertain and had their formal dining-room upstairs. They made their sitting room below, where the shop had started. These were draughty places with no form of heating other than the open fire. Many houses needed open fires in the bedrooms during the winter months. Lighting in Tom's time was by oil lamps. They were fragile to handle and the globes needed to be kept clean. One of the lamps survives to this day.

In many houses lamps like this one were proudly displayed in the parlour or the " good room" as the sitting room was often described.

*Oil lamp which belonged to Tom and Lizzie*

Sometime in the 1920's Tom leased the shop so that he could go to Portrush. Although they had no children of their own they did have the responsibility of Lizzies' five young nieces, whose parents had died young. They ran a boarding house so that the girls could attend Coleraine High school.

A Corner of the East Strand, Portrush.

*Scenes of Portrush*

The shop wasn't the same without him. When the lease was up the departing tenant decided to help himself to the beautiful china that was in the house. Tom was not aware of what was happening. The crates packed with precious goods were carried to the railway line to be transported away. They were placed too near to the track. A passing rail-car hit them and scattered the china into hundreds of little pieces. Years later we found this treasure. It was perfect for playing "wee shops".

*The rail-car sits at Stranorlar Station*

Tom returned to the shop in the late 1930's. By that time he needed an heir to carry on the business. His nephew Charles, my father, was deemed suitable. He was not keen on the idea at first.

*Charles Kee*

He was the fourth generation to be named Charles in the Kee family. His early life was spent on the farm, where there was plenty of hard work. He enjoyed the rough and tumble of a large family and kept in close contact with his siblings all his life.

Like many of his generation before and after, Charlie went to England to find work. He got a job on the building of the Royal Ordnance Munition factory in Chorley, Lancashire. There were 868 employed in the building of the large factory. It took two years from 1937 to 1939 to build.

"Is there owt coming?" was one of the expressions he used to use. "There's nowt for nowt" was another Lancasterian saying he picked up.

Back at home, Charlie found life very different in his uncle's household. There were many rules he wasn't used to at home. "Tom was a hard taskmaster," he would often say. He was quick tempered. However he was very good to his customers. He was too soft at times and people would play on his generosity.

Charlie was 21 years of age when he went to work in the shop in 1934. In later life he would recall the hardships of the "hungry thirties". It was very difficult for the majority of the population to "make ends meet".

*Charlie*

The outbreak of the Second World War in 1939 brought rationing of many products in the shop. Although the Free state remained neutral the effects were felt in the shop.

During the Emergency, as the Second World War was known in Ireland, every individual was issued with a ration book, and rationing continued long after the end of the war. Commodities rationed during the war included tobacco, tea, sugar, flour, soap and clothing.

½ oz of tea or ½ lb of sugar didn't go far in a large family. Customers were always looking for more. It was difficult, as all the tea and sugar had to be accounted for, down to the last ounce. Inspectors came to check up and the shopkeeper was fined if he didn't adhere to the rules.

# CHARLIE TAKES OVER THE SHOP

*Charles Kee*

CHARLES KEE

GENERAL GROCER,

HARDWARE, CHINA & GLASS STORE

MEENAGRAVE, WELCHTOWN,

CO. DONEGAL.

MEMO.

M

My father was delighted when he was able to take over the business. He was very happy to be his own boss. The year was 1942. He had spent 12 years learning the trade.

He was a mild tempered man, quite different from his uncle. He was known as 'Charlie The Shop' as there were a number of Charlie Kees in the district. Jimmy, his younger brother, was sent to help him. Jimmy was a fun-loving lad. He had many young admirers, who would make all sorts of excuses to visit the shop when he was there. Years later he could vividly recall his early life and he would regale us with stories of people and places long forgotten.

Some of the family names that were familiar in the district were - Patton, Kee, Temple, Hume, Bonner, Slavin, McGinty, Arnold, McCreery, Chambers, McCool, McMenamin, McCormick, Dougherty and Boyle, Griffith, Bustard, Slavin, McCreedy, Leeper, McGonigle, Boyce, Carlin, McCrudden, Scanlan, Kelly, Marley, McGowan, Stewart, Cassidy, Cunningham, Donaldson, Blackburn, Heron and Thompson. Most had lived side by side for generations.

*Bother Jimmy who worked in the shop until 1958*

On occasions, Charlie would go to Kee's hotel in Stranorlar to meet a shoe rep who was staying there. A young waitress, by the name of Jennie McClean, caught his eye.

*Wedding day of Charles and Jennie 12th February 1945*

They were married in 1945. It was the beginning of a long and happy marriage that lasted for over 50 years.

This photograph was taken in Strabane by H.F. Cooper.

*Jennie with her children Dorothy, Charles and Pearl*

Jennie never worked in the shop. She was the homemaker. She had great skills with her hands, from making clothes to carpentry work. She loved gardening.

In those days a mother's place was in the home. Very few women in our locality went out to work. In many houses there were also elderly grandparents. Rocking the cradle was a job for an elderly woman sitting in the corner. The woman in the house would also be busy outside as well as inside. An extra pair of hands was useful. Families were large so it wasn't easy feeding many mouths. It was up to the housewife to be resourceful. There was usually a vegetable garden and some fruit. Orchards were still in fashion. The Children Allowance didn't stretch far as can be seen from the book that my father had.

# GROCERIES FOR SALE

My father stood behind the grocery counter ready to serve the customer. There wasn't a fridge or freezer in sight. No wash hand basins or plastic gloves were to be seen. The wooden counter was wide and the goods ordered were laid out in front of the customer.

*This weighing machine was similar to the one we had sitting on the counter in the shop.*

No goods came pre-packed. Everything was weighed in lbs or ounces on the weighing machine on the counter. The filled bags had to be tied with a cord which hung from the ceiling over the counter. It was a skilled job to secure a knot with your thumb. It took a lot of patience to train young fingers in the art of the job.

The weights and measures man visited once a year. It was an anxious time as you could be fined if your weighbridge was not weighing accurately.

# Shopping List

Tea, Sugar and Butter were nearly always the top items on the shopping list.

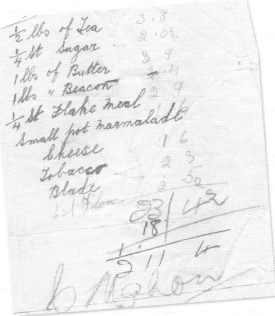

*A shopping list from 1957*

Behind the grocery counter was the tea bin filled with loose tea. I can still remember the smell when the lid was lifted.

Usually the tea was sold by the quarter or half pound. A tea chest held 80 lbs. and was ordered from Baker Wardell & Co., Thomas St., Dublin.

**BAKER WARDELL & CO. LTD.**
76 & 82 THOMAS ST.   DUBLIN 8
A MEMBER OF THE ITM GROUP

INVOICE

MRS. C. KEE,
MILLINAGRAVE,
WELSHTOWN,
CO. DONEGAL.

Nº 13963

TEL. 57081

INVOICE

DATE -8DEC65  NO. 9106

DELIVERY:
RAIL
CGE PD HOME.

| | DATE | REF. | REG. | UNREG. | ORDER NO. | | | |
|---|---|---|---|---|---|---|---|---|
| | 7/12/65 | | X | | 2   158 | | | |
| | 1 Lb | ½ Lb | ¼ Lb | TOTAL Lbs. | PRICE | £ | s. | d. |
| RED CAPITAL. | | 96 | | 96 | 6/- | 28 | 16 | 0 |
| GOLD CAPITAL. | | 6 | 6 | 12 | 6/5 | 3 | 17 | 0 |
| | | | | | | 32 | 13 | 0 |

WHOLESALE   TEA   SUGAR   AND   COFFEE   MERCHANTS
**CAPITAL TEA**

They were a Quaker family and had a large wholesale tea, sugar and coffee company. Their brand of tea was Red Capital and Gold Capital. The stamp on the side of the chest said Ceylon. That was a long way from home. I had seen pictures in my geography book of people out in the fields in tea plantations and often wondered if they had picked our tea.

Empty tea chests were in great demand by customers who had a variety of uses for them. Small animals could be nursed back to health in them beside the fire in the kitchen.

Next to the tea was the sugar bin. Sugar was in big demand. It was sold mostly by the ¼ stone.

Patrick, a loyal customer, was fond of sugar. In the winter he had to walk a long way to the shop. He loved to warm his hands at the fire and greatly appreciated tea served in a bowl. "Can I have six spoonfuls of sugar, please?" he would ask. This was normal practice in many homes.

## Tobacco

Tobacco, for the man in the house, was also essential. It was kept in a drawer in the counter. The tobacco came in long bars and had to be cut with a special knife. 2 oz. was the usual order. Spearman's tobacco came in 8oz. packs. In 1953 2oz tobacco cost 3s.9d.

Chewing tobacco came in a round coil. It was lethal on men's teeth, staining them brown. Even worse were the customers, thankfully few in number, who spat it out on the shop floor. We waited with bated breath for this to happen. They never disappointed. How we hated having to brush the floor afterwards.

We were always fascinated by the blacksmith when he got his tobacco. He would set his pipe on the counter and get his penknife from a pocket in his waistcoat. He would then carve the tobacco into thin strips and rub it between his large hands. Eventually he would fill his pipe and get it lit. A puff of smoke would fill the shop, but it didn't seem to matter. There was an air of contentment about the place.

Another product of tobacco, called snuff, was a favourite of old ladies. Snuff was crushed tobacco leaves and looked a bit like pepper. It was stored in a small drawer and was weighed with a tiny scoop. ½ oz. went a long way. A pinch was the amount you could lift between your index finger and your thumb. It was placed into both nostrils. It seemed to work well for old ladies but only made us sneeze!

Cigarettes were in great demand - Woodbine, Sweet Afton, Players and No 1 tipped, Park Drive, Benson and Hedges Silk Cut. In 1965 the quantity of cigarettes ordered showed how fashionable it was to smoke. 2000 Sweet Afton and 1000 No 1 tipped and 5000 Park Drive plain came from Gallahers in Dublin. I don't know how often this order was placed.

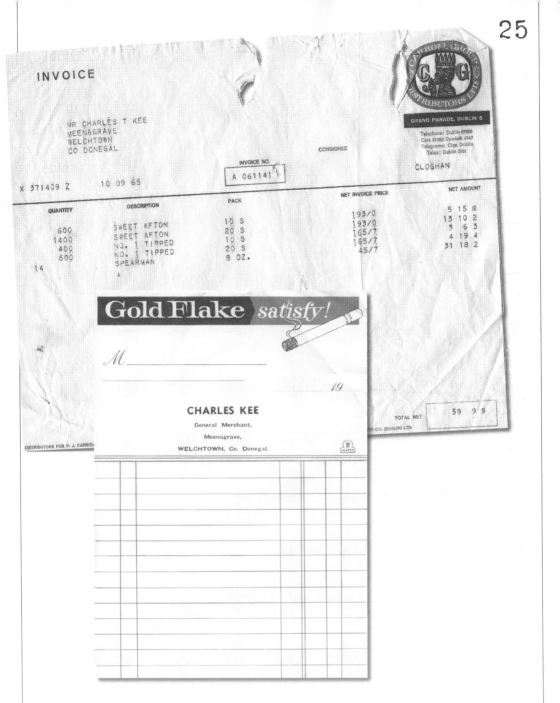

*Gold Flake was advertised on bill heads*

On one occasion Tom rode around the Lake District in England on his bicycle. He stopped at a graveyard to rest and made conversation with an old man who was tending the graves. The man was smoking a pipe. Tom gave him a lecture on the evils of smoking. He didn't mention that he supplied his own customers at home with the evil weed!

# Biscuits

Biscuits were a luxury. They were stored in large biscuit tins belonging to Jacobs. 2s. were charged for these tins and, when returned, the empties were credited. In 1851 two brothers, William Beale and Robert Jacob, started making biscuits in Waterford but later moved to Dublin. Great expansion took place in Dublin and they opened a branch in England. Eventually the Jacob brand became known all over the world.

In our shop the range of biscuits ordered changed very little from month to month - Fig Rolls, Goldgrain, Lincoln Creams, Marie, Irish Wheaten, Custard Creams, Kimberley, Coconut Cream, Rich Tea, Marietta, Mikado, Polo, Kerry Cream and Cream Crackers. Some of these biscuits were more fragile than others. When handled a lot they were inclined to break. This was a great delight to schoolchildren, who could sometimes afford a bag of broken biscuits. What a treat on the way home from school!

*Window display in Blackwood's of Sligo*

# W. & R. JACOB & CO., LTD.

BISCUIT MANUFACTURERS, DUBLIN 8, IRELAND

Telephone: Dublin 53351 (10 Lines). Telegrams: Jacob, Dublin

**INVOICE**

MR CHARLES KEE
MEENAGRAVE
WELSHTOWN P O
CO DONEGAL

L011
YG

A/c. No. 282621015/U/O     DATE 17 FEB 66     INV. REF. 007947

| DESCRIPTION | QTY. | PACK | WEIGHT | PRICE s. d. | VALUE £ s. d. |
|---|---|---|---|---|---|
| CREAM CRACKER | 1 | CB | | 21 2 | 1 1 2 |
| MARIE PKTS | 1 | CB | | 22 2 | 1 2 2 |
| MARIETTA PKTS | 1 | CB | | 17 3 | 17 3 |
| KIMBERLEY | 1 | SQ | 8¼ | 1 11 | 15 10 |
| LINCOLN CREAMS | 1 | SQ | 9¼ | 1 10 | 17 0 |
| COCOANUT CREAM | 1 | SQ | 7 | 1 11 | 13 5 |
| RICH TEA | 1 | SQ | 8¼ | 1 11 | 16 9 |

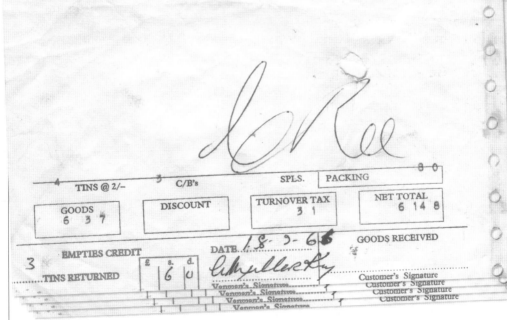

8 0

| 4 TINS @ 2/- | 3 C/B's | SPLS. | PACKING |
|---|---|---|---|

| GOODS 6 3 7 | DISCOUNT | TURNOVER TAX 3 1 | NET TOTAL 6 14 8 |
|---|---|---|---|

3 EMPTIES CREDIT     DATE 18-3-66     GOODS RECEIVED

TINS RETURNED     £ s. d.     6 0

Venman's Signature
Venman's Signature
Venman's Signature
Venman's Signature

Customer's Signature
Customer's Signature
Customer's Signature
Customer's Signature

# 23

## The Sweetie Jars

In the centre of the back wall, behind the counter, there were two shelves lined with shiny glass jars. The bright coloured sweets were there to tempt the customer. In earlier times a poke of sweets was a real luxury -ten toffees for 1d. My father would often show us how to make a poke. It was more difficult than it looked.

*I have kept this poke that my father made for me years ago.*

The invoice from Oatfields in Letterkenny shows the large variety of sweets on the market. A quarter of sweets was the usual order. Conversation lozenges were popular. As the boiled sweets were not individually wrapped they tended to stick together at the bottom of the sweetie jar. Our cousin Valerie remembers having to pour hot water over the sweets to release them. They couldn't be sold but they could be eaten by little cousins who were visiting!

There were also bars of chocolate including Dairy Milk, Fruit and Nut, Crunchies and Rolo. Toffee bars were sore on the teeth. However, the school dentist had no qualms about extracting damaged teeth.

I will never forget the episode with the nougat bars - those lovely chewy bars with pink and white stripes. We were playing in the corn field at the back of the shop with a large group of friends. Someone suggested that we needed a treat from the shop. My sister was volunteered for the job. The wholesaler had delivered an order earlier in the day. A box of nougat was still sitting on the counter. It was too tempting to pass. We had a great feast. All too soon the bars in the box were gone. Eventually the missing box had to be accounted for and we had to own up to the crime. We were severely reprimanded and sent to bed. The other culprits went home unpunished. It wasn't fair!

Jelly was a popular dessert in the country. Lamb Bros from Dublin had table jellies in many flavours - greengage, lemon, lime, orange, pineapple, port wine, raspberry and strawberry. A treat for the working man was rice pudding. The rice was loose and had to be weighed. It needed a steady hand to scoop it from the drawer. Usually stray grains had to be brushed from the counter. My father hated the waste.

# WM. McKinney & Sons Ltd.

## OATFIELD CONFECTIONERY WORKS, LETTERKENNY

Mr. Charles Keo
Seagrave,
Welchtown.

DB No. 9930 ___ Outers    Despatched   "8 NOV 1969"
___ Cartons

| JARS | TINS | BOXES | LBS. | ORDER NO. | PER VAN | OUTERS | PRICE | | |
|------|------|-------|------|-----------|---------|--------|-------|--|--|
| | | | 4 | 9d. per Qr. Butter Macaroons | | | | | |
| | | | 4 | 9d. ,, Orange Chocolate | | | | | |
| | | | 4 | 9d. ,, Glucose Barley Sugar | | | | | |
| | | | 5 | 8d. ,, Menthol & Eucalyptus | | | | | |
| | | | 5 | 8d. ,, Chocolate Satines | | | | | |
| | | | 5 | 7d. ,, Green Isle Selection | | | | | |
| | | | 5 | 7d. ,, Crystal Fruits | | | | | |
| | | | 5 | 7d. ,, Lime & Lemon | | | | | |
| | | | 5½ | 7d. ,, Black Striped Balls | | | | | |
| | | | 5½ | 7d. ,, Orange and Lemon Slices | | | | | |
| | | | 5½ | 7d. ,, Winter Mixture | | | | | |
| | | | 5½ | 7d. ,, Brandy Balls | | | | | |
| | | | 5½ | 7d. ,, Paradise Fruits | | | | | |
| | | | 5½ | 7d. ,, Liquorice Variety | | | | | |
| | | | 5½ | 7d. ,, Dairy Mixture | | | | | |
| | | | 5½ | 7d. ,, Mixed Gooseberries | | | | | |
| 4 | 7 | 8 | 6d. Assorted Boilings. | | 4 12/4 | | 2 | 9 | 4 |
| | 1 | | Eskimo Mints | | 1 9/6 | | | 9 | 6 |
| | | | 5 | 1/1 per Qr. Milk Chocolate Caramels | | | | | |
| | | | 5 | 1/1 ,, Chocolate Favourites | | | | | |
| | | | 5 | 1/1 ,, Emerald Chocolate Caramels | | | | | |
| | | | 5 | 1/- ,, Winter Easers | | | | | |
| | 2 | | 5 | 9d. ,, Colleen De Luxe | | 2 9/10 | | 1 | 1 | 8 |
| | | | 5 | 9d. ,, Butter Macaroons | | | | | |
| | | | 5 | 9d. ,, Orange Chocolate | | | | | |
| | | | 5 | 9d. ,, Glucose Barley Sugar | | | | | |
| | | | 5 | 9d. ,, Eskimo Mints | | | | | |
| | | | 5 | 9d. ,, Lagan Cream Toffee | | | 4 | - | 6 |
| | | | 5 | 9d. ,, Toffee Supreme | | | | | |
| | | | 5 | 8d- ,, Garden Fruits | | Dis 2½ | 2 | - |
| | | | 5 | 8d. ,, Old Time Assortment | | | | | |
| | | | 4 | 7d. ,, Whipped Cream Bon Bons | | | | | |
| | | | 5 | 7d. ,, Family Assortment | | | 3 | 18 | 6 |
| | | | 8 | 7d. ,, Brandy Balls | | | | | |
| | | | 8 | 7d. ,, Black Striped Balls | | | | | |
| | | | 8 | 7d. ,, Winter Mixture | | | | | |
| | | | 8 | 7d. ,, Popular Assortment | | | | | |
| | | | 8 | 7d. ,, Orange & Lemon Slices | | | | | |
| | | | 1½ Doz. 9d. Pick a Packet | | | | | |
| | | | 5 ,, Tiger Bars | | | | | |

# Bread

Beside the biscuit shelf was the press where the bread was kept. It came as a plain or pan loaf delivered by Paddy McNulty who always wore a brown shop coat. His hands were spotlessly clean. The smell of fresh bread in his van was something to be experienced. The bread came unwrapped and unsliced. The loaves were all joined together and had to be prised apart. Paddy used a long hook to pull the drawers of bread from the back of the van. A loaf was always wrapped in tissue paper before being placed in the customer's basket. It was hard to resist pulling a piece from a fresh loaf. It tasted divine. Even better was a slice cut thickly with butter and jam. Jam was sold in the shop. Chapmans was a name associated with good jam. Favourites were blackcurrant, damson, mixed fruit, apricot, Seville orange marmalade, strawberry and raspberry.

Flour was a big seller in the shop. Every household baked their own bread. Shop bread was a luxury. Fresh bread from the griddle was the best way to eat it. Flour came in 4st, 8st or 10st. bags. A 4st. bag cost 17s 6d in 1954; a 10st. bag in 1956 cost £2 and by 1960 the price had risen to £3 11s 6d. This was the size that was normally bought. It took it all to feed a large family. Flake meal and Indian meal were also sold for baking.

# Bacon

*The bacon slicer sat at the end of the grocery counter.*

The bacon slicer was well used. A roll of bacon was placed in the machine. The blade was adjusted to cut thick or thin slices. A roll of 46lb was delivered by Jim Hannigan. Some mince was also purchased.

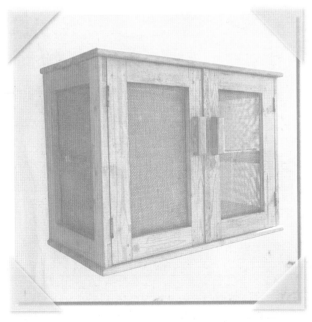

*The Meat Safe*

It was difficult to keep these items cool in warm weather as large bluebottles would appear. The meat safe in the back store was the only form of refrigeration in the shop. It consisted of a wooden cupboard. The door was covered in mesh with holes small enough to keep the flies at bay. Times have certainly changed.

In 1954 Eddie Gibbons bought 11½ lb of bacon at 2/6 a lb. Thomas Doherty bought 9lbs of smoked bacon for £1 8s 6d. in 1953.

Bacon fried with cabbage was very much part of the staple diet of country folk. It was hard to beat.

REG. NO. 9/J/28752   INVOICE

# J. HANNIGAN & SONS

BACON, COOKED HAM & SAUSAGE WHOLESALERS

## STRANORLAR, CO. DONEGAL   No. 18591

Telephone: BALLYBOFEY 140

Sold to _Mr 6 Hree_   Date _14/10/19 68_
_Meenagrave_

| No. | | | | Lbs. | @ | £ | s. | d. |
|---|---|---|---|---|---|---|---|---|
| 1 | Rolls | L | m/c | 46 | | 8 | 12 | 6 |
| | " | | | | | | | |
| | " | | | | | | | |
| | Sides | | | | | | | |
| | " | | | | | | | |
| | Middles | | | | | | | |
| | Gammons | | | | | | | |
| | Cooked Hams | | | | | | | |
| | " | | | | | | | |
| | Sausages | | | | | 4 | 8 | |
| 2 | Mince | | | | | 8 | 14 | 2 |
| | Lard | | | | | | 4 | 5 |
| | | | | | | 9 | 1 | 7 |

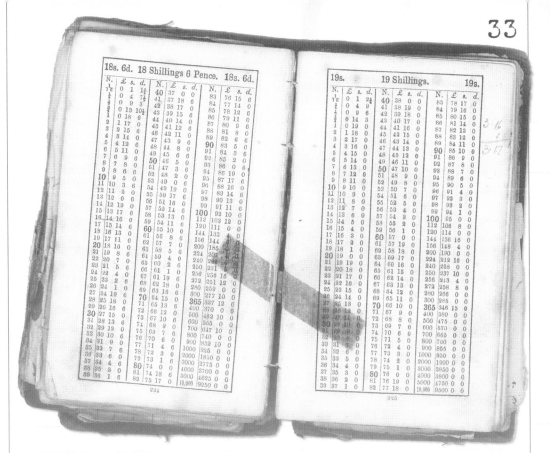

*The Ready Reckoner which could calculate anything that my father needed.*

Mental arithmetic was very useful when my father was totting up the bills. We were amazed at how he could run his eye up and down a page and calculate how much he was owed. Then he would ask us to check it for him. It took us much longer to do the sums and we found he was always right. Weights and measures were important too. They were trickier to learn than the tables. My father was able to gauge how much to cut for 2oz. of tobacco or how much sugar it took for a 2lb. bag. He prided himself in his accuracy.

A number of essential items were not stocked in the shop. Milk was never needed as the local farmers supplied it to their neighbours. It never came in a bottle only in a tin can. A lot of vegetables were grown in most households so there was little need for them in the shop. If visitors were coming tomatoes were good to have with ham and homegrown lettuce.

I remember once, a fight broke out between schoolchildren on the road. One young lad burst into the shop, grabbed a handful of tomatoes and started pelting his opponents with them. My father was livid.

# HARDWARE

*Early morning, the shutters are still on the shop windows*

The first job in the morning was to remove the shutters from the two shop windows. There were three shutters on each side held in place by an iron bar across the centre of the window. The shop opened promptly at 9am. Closing time was flexible, usually 10pm or 11pm on a Saturday night. It was a long day.

There was a little window in the kitchen overlooking the shop. A bell rang when the latch on the inner door was lifted. We usually had a peep to see who was there. The customer would proceed to the grocery counter and sit on the bench for a chat.

*Harvest Time*

First the weather was discussed. It was mostly too warm, too cold, too windy or too wet. Could the hay be saved? Would the corn ever ripen? Were the potatoes under water as the river flooded? Was the blight bad this year? Did anyone ever remember a worse summer?

Charlie McCready was the man to ask. He knew everything about the weather. "Is it going to be good today?" we would ask him. Charlie grew willow to make baskets. He could tell by the signs in the sky and the direction of the wind what was going to happen. If the swallows flew low over the field or the earthen floor was damp and the crickets were chirping in the hearth it was a sign of rain. If a salmon jumped up straight out of the water or a cat sat with its back to the fire that was a sign of a storm. Charlie was never wrong.

*Charlie McCready*

The weather was of paramount importance to the farmer. Most of the customers were involved with mixed farming. Many grew potatoes and cereals. They kept pigs and hens. They milked cows and made butter.
It was a labour intensive business dependant to a large extent on the weather.

Items in the shop reflected the demand from the customer. Every season of the year had to be catered for. Before mechanisation hand tools were used. For hay making, pitchforks, rakes, and scythes were essential. Spades and shovels were needed for all sorts of work around the farm. Manure forks, hay knives and 1¾ lb. German hunter hatchets were on the shopping list. McMahon Ballybofey spades were popular costing 206s. each in 1964.The price had fallen to 196s. in 1965. Irish ash spade and shovel handles were in big demand. They often broke under pressure from the ground or the handler was too rough. A Pierce slasher was a dear commodity at £1 5s 3d. A 3 cubic ft. rubber-tyred wheelbarrow cost £3 14s. It was lighter than the wooden variety that had been used for generations. In the autumn a 10-prong potato fork was useful.

Many of these items were lined up against the wall of the shop on "the street" as we called it. No one was aware of health and safety issues in those days.

The hardware counter was at the other side of the shop.

A wooden counter similar to the grocery one was filled with numerous items of hardware.

In the 1950's there would be a tilley lamp on the counter. It was an upgrade from an oil lamp. It provided a lot more light, which was better for doing needlework or homework. However it needed a mantle. It was a tricky business changing the mantle. One touch of the fine guaze was enough to put a hole in it. They cost 4s 6d a dozen.

Behind the counter was the shelving where the delph was stored. Rows of cup hooks displayed plain white everyday ware. Blue ribbon was very fashionable. On the shelving sets of china were on display, also mantel clocks, alarm clocks, knives, forks and spoons. Spools of thread, and little packets of needles shaped liked a vase of flowers, were needed for all the mending work. It was easy to tear trousers when crossing a barbed wire fence or rip a jacket climbing over a gate.

Items for the school pupils lined the counter. Exercise books and pencils, rubbers, sharpeners, rulers and fountain pens, ink. Blotting paper was always in big demand.

*Cousin Patricia Allerston joins Pearl and Dorothy outside the shop.*

It is interesting to see the items for sale in the shop window.

In the 1960's aluminium utensils were coming on the market. As hearth fires were being replaced with modern solid fuel cookers so the black pots and pans were dumped outside in barns and behind ditches where they lay for many years. Little did people know that one day they would become so sought after by antique collectors.

Along the top shelf in the picture there is a range of aluminium items including teapots of various sizes.

On the middle shelf are the fancy goods. China tea sets with a pattern were sought after. A half tea set comprising six cups saucers and plates made a great wedding present. It was a prized possession by the new bride and was used on important occasions only. Many were displayed in the china cabinet in the good room.

There was great excitement when McCallig's large van arrived at the shop. They were wholesale fancy goods importers from Claremorris in Co. Mayo. How we loved to get into the van and see all the new items that had been added to the stock. The salesman would unwrap items of glass and china for my father to see. The long list of items that he bought in 1965 can be seen in the invoice, from glasses and mantel clocks to canteens of cutlery and kettles. My father would take orders if wedding presents were needed. I'm sure the 21-piece tea set that was on the list would have been ordered for a present. It cost him £2 10s 0d. A canteen of cutlery was slighter more expensive at £2 11s 6d.

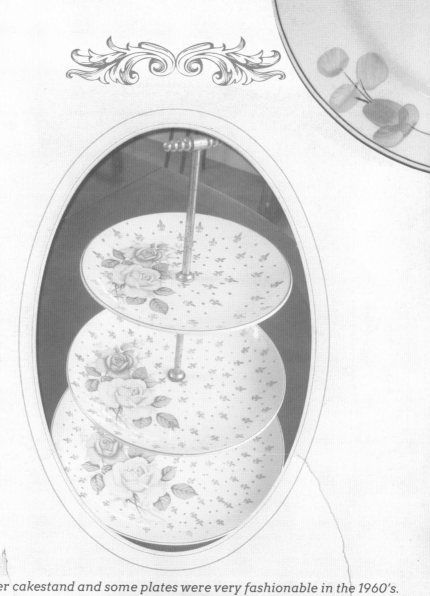

*A three-tier cakestand and some plates were very fashionable in the 1960's.*
*They came from McCallig's van*

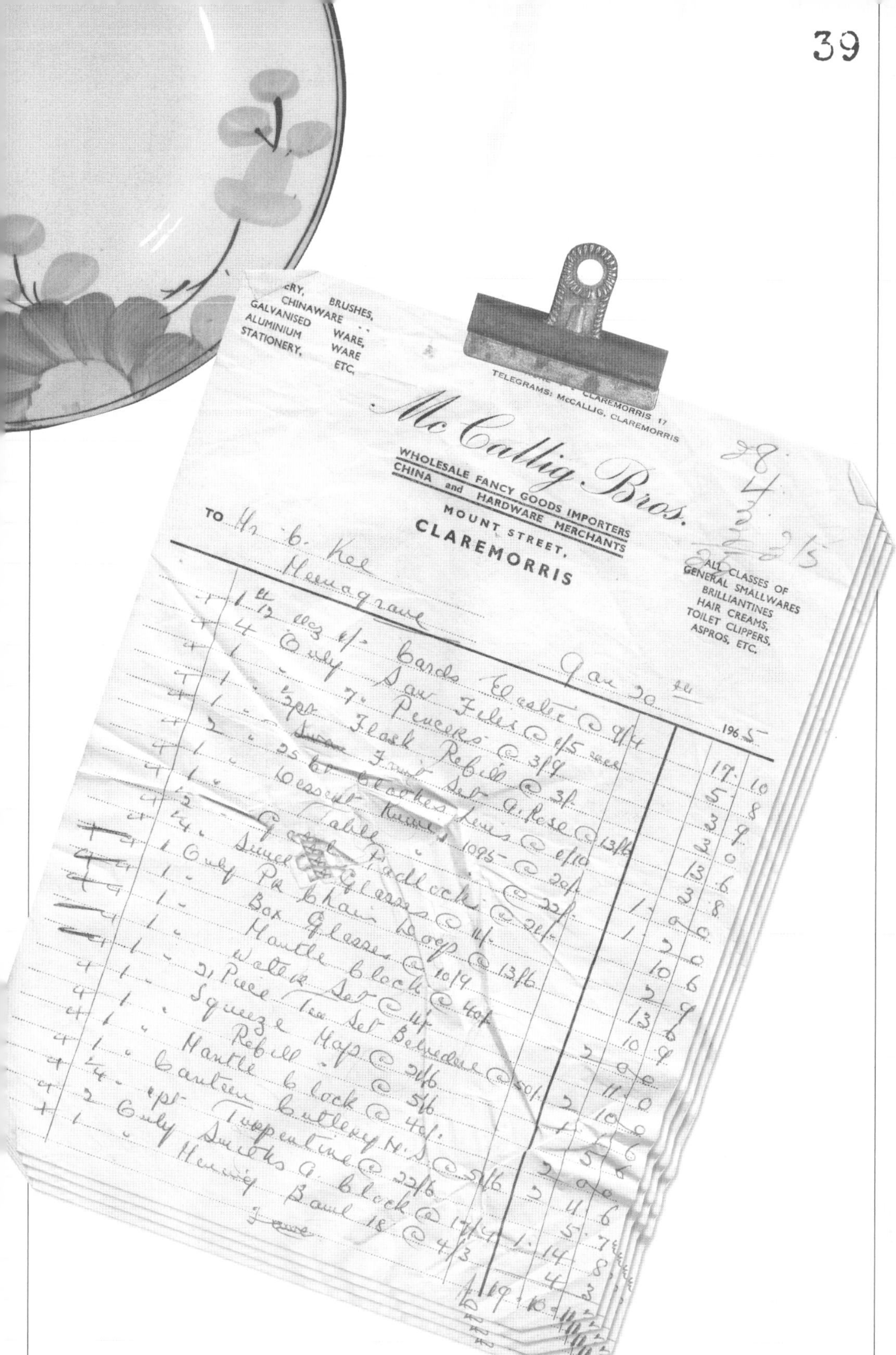

CRY, BRUSHES,
CHINAWARE
GALVANISED WARE
ALUMINIUM WARE
STATIONERY, ETC.

TELEGRAMS: McCALLIG, CLAREMORRIS

CLAREMORRIS 17

*Mc Callig Bros.*

WHOLESALE FANCY GOODS IMPORTERS
CHINA and HARDWARE MERCHANTS
MOUNT STREET,
CLAREMORRIS.

ALL CLASSES OF
GENERAL SMALLWARES
BRILLIANTINES
HAIR CREAMS,
TOILET CLIPPERS,
ASPROS, ETC.

TO Mr. G. Kee

Hanagrane

Jan 30          1965

There was always a need for tin cans. Tinsmiths would travel the length and breadth of the country calling at farms along the way. Once a year John the tinker came to our parts. He was John Doherty. He would come into the shop and talk to my father. He was a quietly spoken man. He would buy the tin in the shop and go outside to a bank further up the road. There he would make as many tins as my father had ordered. He didn't like anyone looking at what he was doing. The cans were filled with water and tested in the backyard before he was paid any money.

John Doherty was one of the leading fiddle players in Ireland. We knew nothing about this until years later. Every year in Donegal there is a festival in his memory.

*John Doherty*

This picture was painted on tin bought in the shop by another tinsmith. It shows Altnapaste in the background and the railway of the wee Donegal line to Glenties on the right of the picture. Our neighbours, the Pattons' house is clearly visible. Move your eye to the centre of the picture. This was my father's shop.

| Utensil Number. | Description | Gauge | | | | | |
|---|---|---|---|---|---|---|---|
| | Globe Tea Set | | 2 | 3 | pints | | |
| | | | 8/- | 9/- | each | | |
| 9005 | Teapot | 18 | 2 pint | | | | |
| | | | 7/9 each | | | | |
| 9007 | Hot Water Jug | 18 | 3/6 each | | | | |
| 9008 | Sugar Bowl | 18 | 5/6 each | | | | |
| 9009 | Cream Jug | 18 | | | | | |
| 9010 | Round Tray | 18 | 14 inch 9/- each | | | | |
| 9010/D | „ „ (Dimpled) | 16 | 15 inch 15/- each | | | | |
| 3000 | Coffee Percolator | 16 | 2 pint 16/9 each | | | | |
| 3001 | Coffee Percolator | 16 | 3 pint 20/6 each | | | | |
| 4000 | Round H.W. Bottle | 22 | 2 pint 4/9 each | | | | |
| 4001 | Kidney H.W. Bottle | 18 | 2 pint 8/6 each | | | | |
| 7000 | Billy Can | 22 | 2 pint 6/6 each | | | | |
| 7000/M | Milk Can | | 3 | 5 | 8 | 12 | 14 pints |
| | 3, 5, 8 pts. | 18 | 7/9 | 9/6 | 11/9 | 19/6 | 22/6 each |
| | 12, 14 pts. | 14 | | | | | |
| 7001 | Porringer: | | 2 | 3 | 4 | 6 | pints |
| | 2, 3, 4 pts. inner | 18 | 10/6 | 11/9 | 14/3 | 21/- | each |
| | outer | 18 | | | | | |
| | 6 pt. inner | 18 | | | | | |
| | outer | 16 | | | | | |
| 7002 | Porringer: | | 17/- | 19/6 | 22/6 | 29/6 | each |
| | 2, 3, 4 pts. inner | 16 | | | | | |
| | outer | 15 | | | | | |
| | 6 pt. inner | 16 | | | | | |
| | outer | 14 | | | | | |
| 7003 | Fitall Steamer | 22 | 6/9 each | | | | |
| 7003/C | Fitall „ & Cover | 22 | 9/- each | | | | |
| 7004 | Colander 9" | 22 | 6/9 each | | | | |
| | „ 14" | 12 | 47/6 each | | | | |

| Utensil Number. | Description | Gauge | | | | | | |
|---|---|---|---|---|---|---|---|---|
| 7005/S | Fish Frier Steel Handle | 18 | 3" deep | | | | | |
| | | | 13/- each | | | | | |
| 7005/B | Fish Frier Bakelite Handle | 18 | 3" deep | | | | | |
| | | | 15/3 each | | | | | |
| 7006/S | Fish Frier Steel Handle | 14 | 4" deep | | | | | |
| | | | 18/- each | | | | | |
| 7006/B | Fish Frier Bakelite Handle | 14 | 4" deep | | | | | |
| | | | 21/- each | | | | | |
| 7007 | Frypan 9", 10", 11" | 18 | 9 | 10 | 11 | 12 | inche |
| | 12" | 16 | 5/6 | 6/6 | 7/6 | 10/3 | each |
| 7008 | Frypan | 14 | 9 | 10 | 11 | 12 | 14 inche |
| | | | 10/- | 11/9 | 12/6 | 15/- | 20/6 each |
| 7009/NS | Non-Stick Frypan | | 10 | 11 | inches | | |
| | | | 26/3 | 27/6 each | | | |
| 7010 | Omelette Pan | 15 | 6 | 8 | inches | | |
| | | | 7/3 | 9/6 | each | | |
| 7011 | Maslin | 16 | 12 | 14 | 16 | inches | |
| | | | 24/- | 28/6 | 35/- | each | |
| 7013 | Maslin | 12 | 36/6 | 41/6 | 47/6 | each | |
| 7014 | Pudding Bowl 3¾" | 22 | 3¼ | 5 | 6 | 7 inches | |
| | „ 5", 6", 7" | 20 | 1/6 | 1/9 | 2/6 | 3/3 each | |
| | „ 8" | 19 | 8 | 9 | 10 | inches | |
| | „ 9", 10" | 18 | 3/9 | 5/3 | 6/- | each | |
| 7014/C | Pudding Bowl Covers | | 5 | 6 | 7 | 8 | 9 | 10 inches |
| | | | 1/9 | 2/- | 2/6 | 2/9 | 3/3 | 3/6 each |
| 7015 | Heavy Pudding Bowl Complete with cover | 16 | ½ 1 2 3 6 lbs. | | | | |
| | | | 3/- 6/3 7/- 9/9 13/9 each | | | | |
| 7019 | Egg Poacher | | 1 | 3 | 9 | holes | |
| | | | 5/- | 9/- | 45/- | each | |
| 7020 | Graduated Measure | 22 | 1 pint 2/9 each | | | | |

Aluminium ware was being introduced as more long-lasting than tin. This catalogue gives an idea of the wide range that was available

Leather was another item to be ordered. John and Jimmy were good customers. Jimmy fixed pans and John repaired shoes. Leather was needed for new soles. Toe plates were good to keep the holes from boots. They were very fond of syrup and bought a lot of it in the shop. Jimmy recycled the tins in many wonderful ways. People would gather in their house bringing shoes to be repaired or collecting them. It was dark inside so John sat by the light of the window. They eventually bought a Tilley lamp in the shop. It gave great light. There was always a bit of banter. Word got out that they kept their money in an oven pot in the room.

"Aye," says Jimmy, "that's right. I had to go out and get a concrete block to keep the lid on the pot!"

# Rural Electrification

One of the greatest debates in the shop took place with the news that the ESB was erecting poles for rural electrification. Many customers declared that it was going to be the ruination of the countryside. Perhaps it was. "Are you getting the electric?" one customer would asked the other in the shop. "It's scandalous what they charging for connection."

Reports about how dangerous electricity was, were circulated, getting bigger and bigger with the telling. They were right in a way as some of the people who were attempting to wire houses were far from qualified.

My father decided he would need it for the shop so he signed up. The wiring cost £1.10.0 for each light fitting. Consequently people only got one or two lights installed. I can remember the day we got the electric in 1957. It was a red letter day. We were so excited that we couldn't stop turning the light switch off and on.

To have light at the flick of a switch instead of oil and Tilley lamps was a step forward. There were still those in the countryside who weren't convinced and who refused to get it. Some were still not connected until the 1970's.

A big innovation was to get the wireless converted to electricity. The wet and dry battery was replaced with wires. Now, listening to Athlone and especially to Saturday theatre, there would be no interruptions by a battery that needed to be recharged.

The wireless kept us in contact with the outside world. We could listen to Radio Luxembourg or when my father wanted to hear the news it was turned over. The McCooeys were a favourite - the forerunner of a soap opera.

The news was filled with all sorts of threats. Nuclear war was the big one at that time.

The Irish government produced a booklet and sent it to every householder in Ireland in 1965. It came to our shop and made grim reading. What to do in the event of a nuclear explosion? Some of the helpful hints were as follows:

Keep the radio tuned into Radio Eireann at all times.
Select a rescue room in your house.
Push the wardrobes over the windows and fill them with earth.
Stock up on food.

If you need to milk cows, build a shelter in the barn and stay with them.

This booklet produced some fierce arguments in the shop among customers. It was debated for many weeks. Some said it was nonsense while others believed every word. Many years later we learned of the appalling effects of a nuclear explosion in Russia.

In November of the same year the assasination of JF Kennedy, President of the United States, was big news. The news was relayed to our shop by some of the customers. Nobody could believe what had happened. There was nothing else to talk about. Every bulletin was listened to and then relayed to others in the shop. JFK was mourned as much in our parish as if he was one of our own.

*Our next door neighbours Hazel, Olive and Iris Patton*

# WATER FROM THE WELL

As we lived in an age before water was piped into the house, spring water was very important. We had no spring of our own but shared with our neighbours, the Pattons. Going to the well was the first job we had to do after coming from school in the evening. The white enamel bucket sat on the bench in the scullery. It was a short walk down the road and through a wooden gate that had to be kept closed at all times because there were usually animals in the field.

The little path led to the spout where the spring water flowed summer or winter. It was the coldest water you ever tasted and sometimes your teeth would tingle after a mouthful of it. The bucket would be filled to the top to allow for spillage on the way back up the hill. Depending how steady your hand was determined whether the bucket was full when you reached the scullery. The water made good tea. A cup hung nearby and was used frequently when we needed a drink.

Rain water was used for all our other requirements. It was great for making your hair shine. No conditioners were needed. It was especially needed for Monday, which was wash-day in most households.

Sunlight soap was sold by the bar or sometimes the half bar. The soap was behind the counter stored in small drawers.

**LIFEBUOY**
*in the home gives health protection to the family*

*Three generations of mothers have relied upon the antiseptic lather of* **LIFEBUOY** *to wash away the germs in dirt.*

2¼d per 4-oz. tablet — 1 coupon *(nett weight when manufactured)*

LEVER BROTHERS, PORT SUNLIGHT, LIMITED

Another soap was Lifebuoy. It was red in colour and had a very distinct smell.

Next an order would come for washing soda. It was lethal on the hands but necessary for the heavily-soiled items in the wash. They were soaked overnight and needed careful handling. When the items were washed they were then rinsed with a bag of blue. I could never understand how a bag of blue gave a white appearance to the wash. Two bags of blue were 3d.

When the blankets were washed once a year it was heavy work. It took extra help to rinse them out and put them through the mangle. Then on to the line which needed to be reinforced with extra poles. A watch had to be kept on the weather. It was easy to know when the rain was coming as the mist started on top of Altnapaste.

Robin starch was required for linens. It took endless patience to starch and iron tablecloths which had been embroidered by members of the family. They were a source of pride, a family heirloom that would be passed to the next generation. When detergent came on the market it was hailed as a great breakthrough. On one occasion my cousin Valerie decorated the shop window with boxes of detergent. She remembered that it made a very colourful display. "I don't think your father entirely approved of the idea but he never said a word," she told me 50 years later.

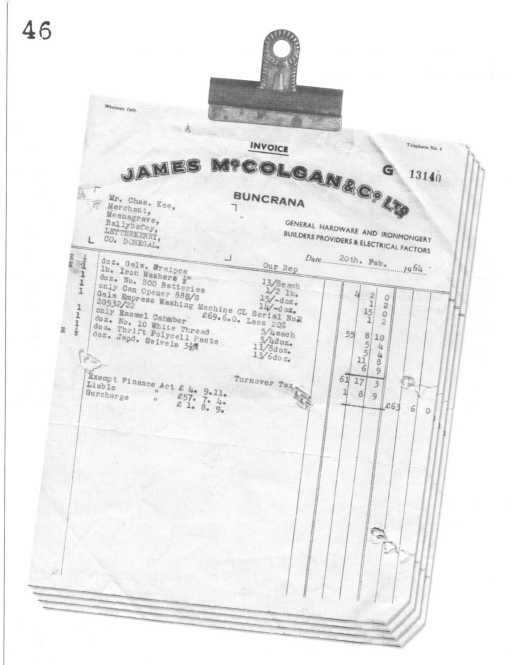

**INVOICE**

Telephone No. 6

# JAMES McCOLGAN & Co. LTD

**BUNCRANA**

G   13140

Mr. Chas. Kee,
Merchant,
Meenagrave,
Ballybofey,
LETTERKENNY,
CO. DONEGAL.

GENERAL HARDWARE AND IRONMONGERY
BUILDERS PROVIDERS & ELECTRICAL FACTORS

Date........20th. Feb.......19 64

Our Rep

| | | | | | |
|---|---|---|---|---|---|
| ½ doz. Galw. Graipes | 13/8each | | 4 | 2 | 0 |
| ½ lb. Iron Washers ½" | 1/2 lb. | | | 1 | 2 |
| 1 doz. No. 800 Batteries | 15/-doz. | | | 15 | 0 |
| 1 only Can Opener 889/S | 14/-doz. | | | 1 | 2 |
| 1 Gala Empress Washing Machine CL Serial No.20532/22 £69.6.0. Less 20% | | | 55 | 8 | 10 |
| 1 only Enamel Cahmber | 5/4each | | | 5 | 4 |
| 1 doz. No. 10 White Thread | 5/4doz. | | | 5 | 4 |
| 1 doz. Thrift Polycell Paste | 11/8doz. | | | 11 | 8 |
| ½ doz. Japd. Swivels 3½" | 13/6doz. | | | 6 | 9 |
| | | | 61 | 17 | 3 |

Exempt Finance Act £ 4. 9.11.
Lisble          "   £57. 7. 4.
Surcharge       "   £ 1. 8. 9.

Turnover Tax          1   8   9

£63   6   0

My mother had longed for a washing machine. She washed clothes for her widowed brother's household as well as her own. Her dream came true on the 20th February 1964 when a Gala Empress Washing machine was purchased from James McColgan and Co., Buncrana. The price - £69 6s 0d less 20% - brought it down to £55 8s 10d. It came with a small mangle on top. She was thrilled with it.

Later that same year an electric iron was purchased for £1 6s 8d.

# Big Houses

Glenmore House, Ballybofey.

There were two big houses in the parish of Kilteevogue. The one nearest to us was called Glenmore. We always referred to it as Glenmore castle. It was a familiar landmark and we passed it every day on our bicycles to school.

The Mackie family, who ran a large foundry in Belfast, bought The Castle in the 1950's and owned it until recent times. They had an account in the shop. My father's ledger makes interesting reading. In 1959, every weekend from August through to December, they must have enjoyed a cooked breakfast before a spot of fishing on the river. The shop order was one or two pounds of bacon, 6 dozen eggs, 2 dozen oranges, packet of cornflakes, 1lb. butter, 2 loaves and ½lb. cheese, occasionally tea was added. Some times tomatoes were ordered if they were in season. The eggs were around 3s 3d per dozen, butter was 4s 4d a lb., oranges were 6d. each, ½lb. cheese was 1s 6d, 1lb bacon was 3s 4d., 2 loaves were 2s 4d., 2lb. sugar was 1s 3d.

In the month of October, 1961, they were supplied with 16 dozen eggs. As there was a farm attached to the house a lot of hardware was also ordered.

Originally the house was built for the Style family. It is not mentioned in the Ordnance Survey Memoirs of 1836 so it must be of a later date. The family were already in Cloghan, and Glenmore was built for a junior member of the family. It was a house built for the gentry, who lived a life far removed from the majority of the population. There were many such families in the area with which to associate. Mrs. Style was a daughter of Mr. Cochran who owned Edenmore, outside Stranorlar. The Styles had two sons and five daughters. Both boys died in their early 20's. Charles, the eldest son, died of consumption in 1845.

There were two gate lodges to Glenmore. The one we knew best was where the McKenna family lived. We knew Mrs. McKenna, her son Gerald, and daughter Mary. She came often to the shop. I remember she always wore a headscarf tied under her chin. She and my father had good chats. We often looked up the avenue and pleaded with our father to take us up to the big house. "We would be trespassing," he said "we don't want to be caught doing that, now do we?"

Uncle Jimmy used to tell us stories of when he went to work in the garden at the age of 14. Hamilton Brown occupied the castle at the time. There were 11 people employed in the garden. They grew all sorts of vegetables and fruit. They had a large greenhouse where they grew exotic fruit he had never seen before. The lawnmower was large and pulled by a horse. It was his job to cut the grass.

The Herdmans of Sion Mills were the next owners. They used it as a fishing lodge, as a good stretch of the River Finn was included in the estate. Jim Saunders, an Englishman, was employed as a land steward. I remember his beachwagon sailing up and down the road and often stopping at the shop for a top-up of cigarettes. There were a number of people employed on the estate. Willie Patton, our neighbour and Mattha Kee, the Roundknowes, worked three days each. Norman Kee and his cousin Jim, as young lads with Paddy and Liam Doherty, were employed on the farm. There was a lot of work to do. One job was cutting trees which were auctioned for posts. Later, Thomas McCreery was employed on the estate and was there until recently.

The maids would arrive in the shop in the beachwagon to place an order, which was then delivered to the castle.

Cloghan Lodge, Ballybofey.

The other big house was Cloghan Lodge, which was the ancestral home of the Style family.

A Millburn family, a father and two daughters, Angela and Pauline, came to live in Cloghan Lodge. We knew little about them as they kept very much to themselves. They did not have an account in the shop. Their great hobby was fishing and, as they owned the fishing rights on the river, they had plenty of places to fish. A favourite was Martin's pool, which was accessed through our uncle's land They parked their car at the shop and would stride down past our clothes line, through the railway line to the river beyond. They always returned with a large fish in the bag.

My sister once asked if she could have one and they agreed that the next one they caught was for her. It never came.

Pauline was a great lover of nature. She once visited Welchtown school and presented each of the pupils with a large scrapbook. She asked us to find pictures of animals and birds and stick them in the book. I have still got mine over 50 years later.

In later life I was to learn that their father was a barrister and a Lieutenant in the Royal Highlanders in the First World War. Their mother was Scottish and died when Angela was 9 years old. Their grandfather was Sir John Davidson Millburn, who made his fortune in shipping and coal in Northumberland. They were able to live by private means.

They relocated to the Isle of Man in the late 1960's and my father visited them there in the 1970's while on holiday. "The old man was so glad to see me," my father told us afterwards. " He was greatly interested in hearing about what was happening in Donegal and asking about the people he knew."

Angela passed away in 2012.

Cloghan Lodge is still in existence, but sadly Glenmore Castle has been demolished.

*A view of Welshtown with the church in the foreground*

# In Sickness

Sickness touched the lives of most people in the community. If a doctor was required the news would spread rapidly to the shop. "They were on their last legs" was a great expression. A daily update on the patient was given in the shop. TB was a great scourge in the country.

In 1939 Tom lost his beloved wife to the disease. She had been ill for a year. Doctors were called only in times of emergency. On many occasions my father was called upon to get the doctor as he had a car. The telephone was usually only in the post office. Our nearest was Welshtown PO. In many emergencies my father would leave the shop and drive the 5 miles to Stranorlar to inform the doctor about someone in the district who needed attention. The doctor in question was Dr. Fred Kee.

Another doctor I remember was Dr. Nancy, who lived in Cloghan.

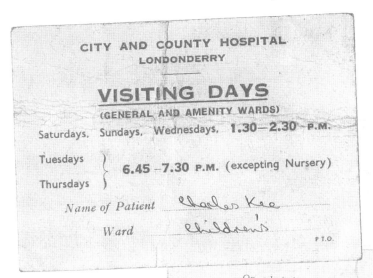

A visiting card had to be produced when visiting a patient.

*Dr. Fred Kee with his wife*

# THE MEDICINE CABINET

Every grocery shop had a medicine cabinet. Ours had glass shelves with a variety of medicines displayed on them. Cough No More was a great cough bottle. It was widely used. John Mortimer, wholesale druggists, were the sole makers of Cough No More. It was advertised as the perfect cough remedy.

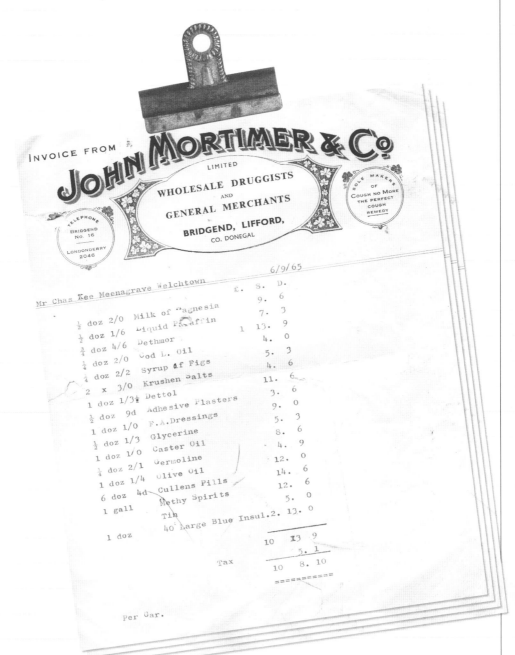

INVOICE FROM

## John Mortimer & Co.

LIMITED

WHOLESALE DRUGGISTS
AND
GENERAL MERCHANTS

BRIDGEND, LIFFORD,
CO. DONEGAL

TELEPHONE
BRIDGEND
No. 16

LONDONDERRY
2046

SOLE MAKERS
OF
COUGH NO MORE
THE PERFECT
COUGH
REMEDY

6/9/65

Mr Chas Kee Meenagrave Welchtown

| | | £. | S. | D. |
|---|---|---|---|---|
| ½ doz 2/0 | Milk of Magnesia | | 9. | 6 |
| ½ doz 1/6 | Liquid Paraffin | | 7. | 3 |
| ¾ doz 4/6 | Dethmor | 1 | 13. | 9 |
| ½ doz 2/0 | Cod L. Oil | | 4. | 0 |
| ¼ doz 2/2 | Syrup of Figs | | 5. | 3 |
| 2 x 3/0 | Krushen Salts | | 4. | 6 |
| 1 doz 1/3½ | Dettol | | 11. | 6 |
| ½ doz 9d | Adhesive Plasters | | 3. | 6 |
| 1 doz 1/0 | F.A.Dressings | | 9. | 0 |
| ½ doz 1/3 | Glycerine | | 5. | 3 |
| 1 doz 1/0 | Caster Oil | | 8. | 6 |
| ¼ doz 2/1 | Germoline | | 4. | 9 |
| 1 doz 1/4 | Olive Oil | | 12. | 0 |
| 6 doz 4d | Cullens Pills | | 14. | 6 |
| 1 gall | Methy Spirits | | 12. | 6 |
| | Tin | | 5. | 0 |
| 1 doz | 40' Large Blue Insul. | 2. | 13. | 0 |
| | | 10 | 13 | 9 |
| | | | 5. | 1 |
| Tax | | 10 | 8. | 10 |

Per Car.

## 54

Also in the cabinet - Cullen's Pills, Vaseline, Iodine, Milk of Magnesia, Blue Insulin, Vick, Glucose, Rennies, Germolene, Beechams Powders, Zambuk, Liquid Paraffin, Cod Liver Oil, Syrup of Figs, Krusken Salts, Glycerine, Caster Oil, Olive Oil, Boracic Ointment and Warfarin. These products were tried and tested and helped to keep the doctor away.

Another tooth...
and not a tear!

What is it soothes the pain away so quickly from those little gums when Baby's teething?
*A gentle dab of 'Milk of Magnesia'.*
And what is it settles little tummies which can so easily be upset at teething time?
*Again, a little 'Milk of Magnesia'!*
That's why countless mothers call 'Milk of Magnesia' a double blessing at teething time ... Then, of all times, they're never without it.

**'MILK of MAGNESIA'** REGD.

SO SOOTHING — SO SAFE
*4 oz. size 2/- — 12 oz. size 4/-*

Cures were handed down from one generation to the next. A bread poultice was good for drawing out a boil. Vick rubbed on the chest took colds away.

# Absent from work with

# SKIN TROUBLE

## then

# *Germolene*

### ASEPTIC OINTMENT

## works wonders

Germolene cools, soothes, heals—always successful. Skin sufferers will find this worth reading: "My wife, after six weeks absence from work through skin trouble had returned but her work has again affected her and we decided to give your much advertised GERMOLENE a trial, and I AM PLEASED TO SAY IT HAS WORKED WONDERS." *H.M.*, Huddersfield. Now's the time for you to get some Germolene: 1/4 and 3/3 a tin including Purchase Tax. **USE GERMOLENE FOR ECZEMA, IMPETIGO, SORES, PIMPLES, RASHES, BLISTERS, IMFLAMMATION and CHAFING of the SKIN, etc.**

Once a year, bog bean was ordered by my father. As the name implies it came from the bog and had long white roots. It had already been boiled and bottled by the time it arrived in the shop. If the liquid looked bad, the taste was worse. "It's to cleanse your blood," we were told. Who were we to disagree?

A shopping list for a wake makes interesting reading:

September 1958
2lbs. tea
60 Players
6lb. Butter
4½ lb. biscuits
1st. Sugar

As youngsters we would also be affected by a death in the community. Our game at this time would be to re-enact the funeral with a cortege of our own. We would each gather a large stone then cover it in moss and add flowers picked from the hedgerows. We formed a procession down the field to the railway line where we would conduct a service and lay the wreaths side by side. It was our way of taking part in the mourning.

# Country Butter

Home-made country butter was a much sought after item, some butter more than others. Sarah made good butter because her cows grazed on heather. That's what we were told. Sarah was always neat and tidy with her hair in a bun. She generally wore a black shawl and carried a wicker basket to the shop. Her butter was prized among the customers. Wrapped in greaseproof paper, it wasn't easy keeping the butter cool in the summer. In really hot weather the butter was floated in cold water in an enamel basin. Some butter makers were proud to have a stamp of their own to put on top. Making butter was a job for the housewife. A churn was an essential utensil in the farmhouse. In older times the plunge churn was the most common type. It required a lot of hard work and patience. My father sold a more up-to-date churn with a glass jar and handle. It was a real innovation.

Later, butter from the creamery was sold. Margarine was then introduced as a substitute for butter. Stork and Summer County were the most popular brands in our shop.

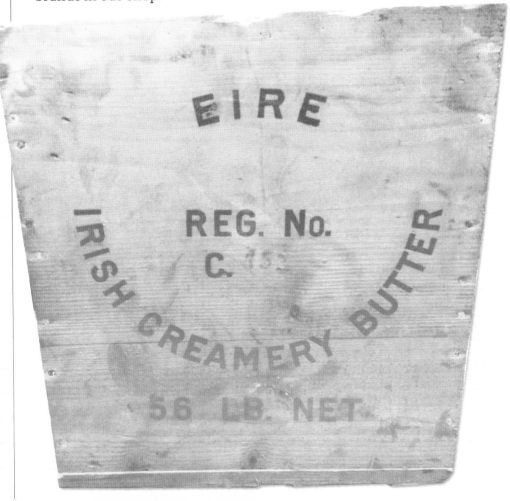

# EGGS

At the back of the shop was an egg store. It was kept cool at all times and was filled with large egg crates.

Eggs were an important commodity for the housewife to earn money. There were hens of various breeds - White Leghorns, Light Sussex and Rhode Island Reds. Bantams were a novelty with their small eggs. Free range wasn't a word that was used in those days. But hens did run freely round the farmyard and some were known to enter the house if the door was left open.

I remember so well being out with my father delivering meal. I looked through the farmhouse door and to my amazement saw hens coming down the stairs. Where had they been? Laying their eggs in the beds? My father couldn't answer my questions.

It was sometimes difficult to find the nests around the yard. Hens liked to hide their eggs in secretive places. Then there was the question of how fresh were they. The eggs arrived in the shop usually in a basket some better packed than others. We fair hated to see dirty eggs arriving as it was our job to clean them. Baking soda was used.

Eggs were then packed into egg sections. A docket was issued which gave the name of the supplier. This was important when the eggs were tested. If found to be bad, notice had to be given to the housewife. How my father hated having to tell the offending party. It was a terrible slur. "Now Charlie, you know I have always good eggs. You must have made a mistake." Charlie never turned the word on them.

A new era came when it was decided that hens would produce more eggs if kept in deep litter.

The eggs were packed in crates of 30 dozen and sent to Honeyfords in Lifford.

Eggs usually helped to pay the grocery bill.

The meal for the hens was ordered in the shop. A bag of Layer's mash cost £1.16s in 1956 and was needed if the hens were to lay well. Half a stone of Chick mash was 2/6d.

*It was a real treat for my two cousins from London, Doreen and Pat Barrett, to feed the chickens. Notice there is a goose in the picture.*

There was always a goose and a gander about the farmyard too. The gander was as good as a guard dog and took great pleasure in hissing and running at anybody who crossed his path. His evil look was enough to send small children scurrying in the other direction.

*A goose and gander patrolling their territory in my grandmother's yard*

*The Hume sisters*

# Potato Buying in the Shop

My father bought potatoes in bulk, which were sent to Dublin.

In one of his black books he records various dates in 1947 and 1948 when he sent potatoes to J. Lightfoot and Sons, Dublin. They were potato merchants and had a wholesale fruit and vegetable business until 2010.

He also records the names of the people who supplied the potatoes

21st Nov 1947.

| | |
|---|---|
| Mick McMenamin | 2 tons |
| Joseph Arnold | 2 tons |
| Tommy Kee | 2 tons |
| William Kee | 4 tons |
| Packy Patton | 2 tons |

12th February 1948 he sent 6 ton of Pinks, 4 ton of Gladstones and 2 ton of Victors.

Carriage had to be paid at 3/6 per ton and amounted to £1 15s 0d for 10 ton. Norman Dennison usually transported the potatoes. This entailed calling at the various farms which took quite a lot of time as the bags had to be carried on their backs from the barns to the lorry. It was heavy work.

Another firm called C. Dodd and Sons also bought potatoes. 9 ½ tons were sent on the 29th April 1948. On the 4th May 1948 he was paid £123 10s 0d - £13 a ton.

Some of the names of the potato growers recorded were-
Elias Griffith, Pat McCrudden, C. McGlynn, Wm. Kee (policeman), Toms Charley, Robert Kee, Joe Ferguson, Frank Harkin, Jim Kee (The Hill), C. Herron, Wm. McCreedy, Jas. Kee (Roundknows), P. McNamee, Tommy Kee, Matt Kee (Welshtown), C. Gallagher and J. Temple, J, McClean, P. McDermot, A. Gallagher, Jas. Arnott, A. Blackburn, Packy Patton.

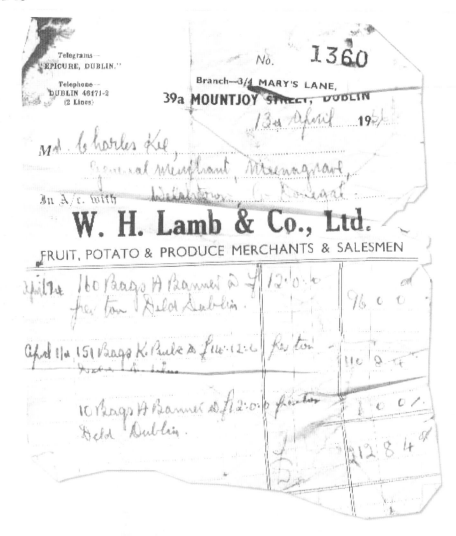

My father continued to buy potatoes right up until 1968. When he sold potatoes to Lamb and Co., it was always an anxious wait as sometimes the potatoes were turned down. They had a very exacting standard and were hard to please.

# Blackberry Picking

Blackberry picking was an occupation for the young. It was their only chance to earn a bob or two. Blackberries were in abundance over 50 years ago. A number of large empty barrels would be delivered from Troughtons in Portadown. It wasn't difficult to get them filled when word got out. Buckets of blackberries would arrive at the shop daily. They were weighed and eager young faces would await the verdict of their crop. Some of the blackberries would be too green, others over-ripe and had to be turned away. Yet others tried the trick of adding water to the bucket to add weight to their blackberries. There was great rivalry in who could earn the most. Secrecy surrounded the many good places to find blackberries. People were prepared to travel distances to get the best of the crop. Many arrived at the shop with purple-stained hands.

One girl told me that she wanted to get to a dance in the Butt Hall. Blackberry picking was her only hope. She had a lot of picking to do. She was over the moon when my father handed her 2s 6d, the exact amount that she needed for the dance.

*Norman, Charlie, Tommy-John and
young Charlie Kee*

# VISITORS

In the summer the news of visitors arriving brought a frenzy of activity. People who had emigrated wanted to come home for their holidays. Most people came from England but some came from America.

Top priority in the district was to get the old homestead looking its best. A coat of paint or whitewash was needed for the house, barns and anything that could be painted. Snowcem was also popular. The colours were white or grey.

Whitewash had been used on cottage walls for generations. Over a hundred years ago Sir T. Charles Style, in Cloghan Lodge, encouraged his tenants to keep their houses clean. He granted £2 to the poorer classes for whitewash. A large brush was stocked in the shop for the job. It cost 2s 9d in 1962. It was a messy business, as the whitewash would spark in all directions, over windows, down drain pipes and even in the flowerbeds. If the wind was blowing then it got into hair, clothes and footwear. We could easily tell in the shop who was busy whitewashing.

Next came the spring cleaning. Every corner had to be tackled. Distemper was used on the interior walls. It was of a chalky nature and could easily rub off on good clothes. Distemper was sold by the packet. 4lb of distemper was 5s 6d. in 1954.

Wallpaper was also stocked in the shop with new patterns every year. I can remember birds and flowers with stripes. It wasn't easy getting it to match up on uneven walls. The good room looked better papered, as well as the bedrooms. Each roll of paper had a line up both sides that had to be cut off before the paper could be matched. This was a time-consuming job. Four rolls of wallpaper cost Master Campbell 18s in 1960. To finish off, a border was stuck to the paper, next to the ceiling. This covered up any blemishes. Ten yards of border could be bought for 1s 8d.

Many kitchens were painted using two colours. The top half was a lighter colour and the bottom half darker. It wasn't easy to get the halfway mark level. Kitchen cupboards were freshened up with gloss paint mixed with turpentine. It created a toxic odour in the house. Tables and chairs were painted the same colour. Red or blue was a favourite colour. It brightened the interior no end. Paint was sold by the lb. and gallon.

Different size brushes 1", 1½", 2", 2½", 3", were available.

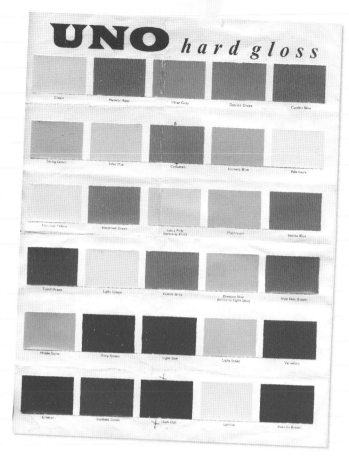

From this colour chart there was a nice range of colours to choose from but the darker colours were generally picked when there were patches of damp to be covered.

The visitors would always come to the shop to talk to my father. We couldn't wait to hear their stories of far-off places. The Americans wore bright colours. We tried to talk with a drawl like they did. New York seemed a million miles away. We wanted to hear about skyscrapers and what they were really like. "Was it true you could fry an egg on the sidewalk?" we would ask. "Sure," was the reply.

How much you could earn was always included in the tall stories. We were envious of the life they painted. Was it as rosy as it seemed? We would never know.

Even closer to home it was amazing the number of people who returned with fancy accents. It was a sad fact of life that many young people had to leave in search of work. Work was plentiful in England. We heard stories of how you could walk out of one job into another. There seemed to be no shortage of money. It was a big change from life at home.

One young lad recounts his first introduction to England.

"I was out working in the fields helping with the hay. I came in, changed my clothes, got my suitcase and headed to Belfast to catch the boat to Heysham. It was filled with young people like myself. At the other side we all went our separate ways. I boarded a train for Manchester. I watched as the countryside turned more industrial. I could see rows and rows of red-bricked terrace houses. There wasn't much room in the small backyards compared to what we had at home. There were large chimneys everywhere with smoke billowing in all directions. It was hard to cope with the smog. An Irish accent was a drawback as we were all known as Paddies. It took a while to get used to a different way of life.

I got a job that paid £9 a week. It was 1962. I was able to put £5 in a post office account every week. That first Christmas, I bought my ticket to fly home. It cost £16 return flight to Belfast. I then bought myself a new suit at £12 and an overcoat for £18. In my pocket was £100. I was well pleased with myself. It was good to get home for the holidays."

A visitor that we always loved to see was our uncle Jimmy. He had been in England since 1958 but he had lost none of his Irish accent. He was full of fun and would arrive with a bundle of comics. The Beano was a great favourite and we used to fight over who would read them first.

Jimmy loved to see his old friends when he was home. Every night he was out visiting or going to dances and socials. He was always sad when his holiday was over. We missed him too. His laugh was as good as a tonic.

Our London cousins were very energetic. They loved life on the farm and were eager to help. We had never heard of pocket money until they came. Our pay for working was a bottle of Tango. We were happy enough.

Five of our cousins from the north came most summers. One of our cousins, Wilma, started her career in the veranda of our house. She learned to sew there using material from my mother's scrap bag.

*Cousins Wilma and Valerie having fun by the River Finn*

The highlight of the summer was the midnight feast we were allowed to have on the night before our cousins went home. Sweets, crisps and drinks were smuggled from the shop and hidden away for the great feast. Sometimes we couldn't stay awake until the midnight hour which spoiled the whole effect.

In 1963 my mother said goodbye to her nephew Rankin. He was emigrating to Canada. In her papers I found a card he had sent her.

B.O.A.C. "707", Prestwick Airport, Scotland.

AT.1392

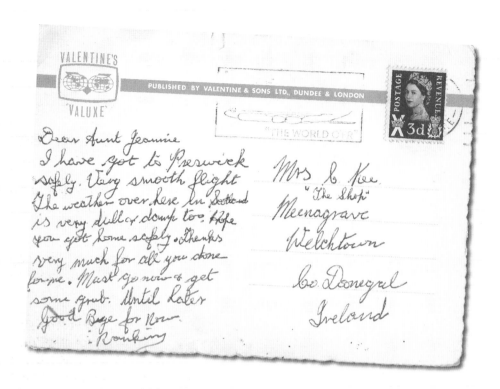

Dear Aunt Jeannie
I have got to Prestwick safely. Very smooth flight. The weather over here in Scotland is very dull or damp too. Hope you got home safely. Thanks very much for all you done for me. Must go now & get some grub. Until Later. Good Bye for Now.
Rankin

Mrs. L. Kee
"The Shop"
Meenagrave
Welchtown
Co. Donegal
Ireland

He never forgot his aunt and sent her regular letters telling about his new life. She in turn would tell him all the news from home.

Hearts at home were heavy when young ones went away. A letter was the most common form of communication and was eagerly awaited. It was expected of those who went away to send some money home. It was also a sign that they were doing well.

We could tell when someone got a parcel from America. It was never mentioned as people didn't want to be thought of as a charity. But we knew as the clothes were brighter than at home. We were sad that one of those parcels never came our way.

# In the Loft

The loft above the shop could be accessed inside by the wooden stairs at the hardware end of the shop. It ran the length of the shop and was used as a meal store.

When the lorries came to deliver the meal they would reverse round the corner of the shop and up the side. The door in the loft was opened and a large hook was lowered and attached to the meal bag. It was then winched up into the loft to be stored. The same happened when customers arrived with their horses and carts. They too reversed up the side of the shop and the meal was lowered on to the cart. We were well warned not to go too close to the open door as it was a 20 ft. drop to the ground below. In the loft there were bags of layers mash, chick mash, linseed, golden drop, scotch corn, bran, oatmeal, maize, corn, flour and flake meal. It was well insulated and kept the meal dry. One of our games as children was to jump from bag to bag in the loft. Often we missed our footing and would fall between the bags. We ended up being covered in dust from head to foot.

Some of the meal was delivered to the customer. It was done after working hours and in whatever car my father was driving. There was a lot of talking done at each stop. We didn't mind as long as we were allowed to do a bit of driving over rough lanes - not on the county road. It was great practice for later when we were the legal age to do so.

*Delivering goods to the customers*

At the far end of the loft was a little room panelled in wood. In earlier times it was the shop-boy's room. It was where my father stored the wellingtons. There was a pungent smell of rubber.

Boots and wellingtons were the main items of footwear worn in the countryside.

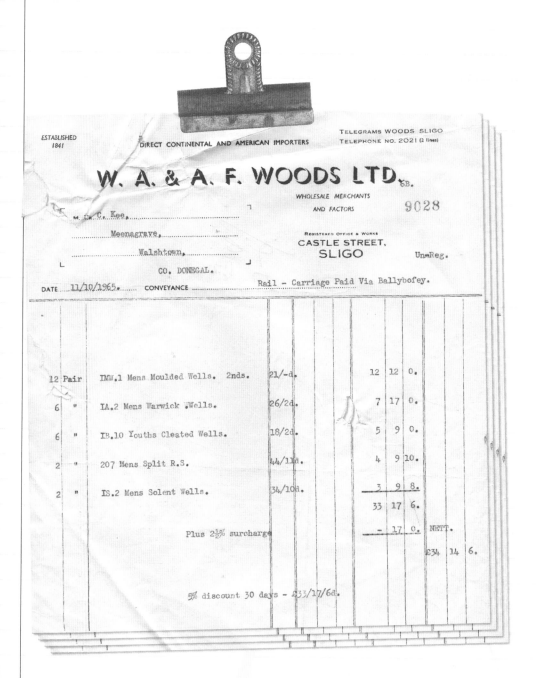

ESTABLISHED 1841

DIRECT CONTINENTAL AND AMERICAN IMPORTERS

TELEGRAMS WOODS SLIGO
TELEPHONE NO. 2021 (2 lines)

# W. A. & A. F. WOODS LTD.SB.

WHOLESALE MERCHANTS
AND FACTORS

9028

M. Mr. C. Kee,

Meenagrave,

Walshtown,

CO. DONEGAL.

REGISTERED OFFICE & WORKS
CASTLE STREET,
SLIGO          Un-Reg.

DATE 11/10/1965.    CONVEYANCE .......... Rail – Carriage Paid Via Ballybofey.

| | | | | | | |
|---|---|---|---|---|---|---|
| 12 Pair | IMW.1 Mens Moulded Wells.  2nds. | 21/-d. | | 12 | 12 | 0. |
| 6 " | IA.2 Mens Warwick Wells. | 26/2d. | | 7 | 17 | 0. |
| 6 " | IB.10 Youths Cleated Wells. | 18/2d. | | 5 | 9 | 0. |
| 2 " | 207 Mens Split R.S. | 44/11d. | | 4 | 9 | 10. |
| 2 " | IS.2 Mens Solent Wells. | 34/10d. | | 3 | 9 | 8. |
| | | | | 33 | 17 | 6. |
| | Plus 2½% surcharge | | | - | 17 | 0. NETT. |
| | | | | £34 | 14 | 6. |

5% discount 30 days – £33/17/6d.

Solent wellingtons were £1.14s 6d in 1953. A pair of child's wellingtons were 15s in 1960.

In the winter thick socks were needed to wear with wellingtons as they were very cold. Men usually folded their long socks over the top. That is how they came to the shop. Often the smell was less than desirable when they were worn all the time. Ladies who wore wellingtons for a long time developed a ring round their legs. It looked bad on a Sunday when they wore nylons, as the mark was clearly seen.
Boots and shoes were also sold in the shop.

A pair of boots cost Samuel McClean £1 19s 11d in August 1960.

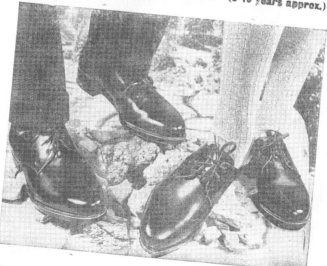

# SQUADRON CADET
## – the hardwearing shoes for boys and youths (8-16 years approx.)

The good-looking school or college cum Sunday shoe with extra hardwearing qualities that boys in this age group demand. Light, flexible, extremely comfortable.

**6 MONTHS WRITTEN GUARANTEE**

| | | | | | | | | |
|---|---|---|---|---|---|---|---|---|
| | | | | May 58 25 Cwt Rfndo @ 20/Cwt | 25 | 0 | — |
| | | | | To Balance £24/ / | | | |
| 8 | 16 | 6 | 9/7/58 | Per John to be taken of spray 2 — | | | |
| 3 | 19 | 0 | | To Cal. £20 | / | / |
| 3 | 2 | 6 | | | | | |
| 2 | 4 | 1 | | (Brought fwd from other Book) | | | |
| | 8 | 0 | 58. April 3rd | 1 Bar 2+2¼ agle Iron. | 1 | 2 | 11 |
| 2 | 16 | 0 | 12th | 2 cuts Grasseed. 86/: perewt | 8 | 12 | 0 |
| | 15 | 0 | | 14 st Corn. 57/- per St. | 3 | 10 | 0 |
| | 6 | 6 | May 7th | 4 lbs Alsyke & white Clover | | 11 | 6 |
| | 11 | | | 4 lbs Wild White | | 5 | 4 |
| | | | | 2 cwt N. Lime | 2 | 2 | 0 |
| | 11 | 6 | | 6 tons Lime | 4 | 13 | 0 |
| 2 | 4 | 0 | | 1 bn Super. | 12 | 16 | 0 |
| | 14 | 0 | | 2 tons Potatoe manure | 34 | 0 | 0 |
| 2 | 5 | 0 | | 4 cwts Potash | 3 | 16 | 0 |
| 10 | 17 | 0 | | 6 cwts Ammonia | 6 | 3 | 0 |
| 2 | 2 | 0 | | 3 cwts Lime (White) | 3 | 3 | 0 |
| 2 | 16 | 0 | | 1 cwt Lime | 1 | 1 | 0 |
| | 14 | 4 | | 4 cwt Potatoe manure. | 3 | 8 | 0 |
| 1 | 7 | 0 | 23rd | 4 lbs Bacon. | | 12 | 6 |
| | 16 | 4 | | Broom | | 5 | 9 |
| 2 | 16 | 0 | July | 2 Cuts Copper | 6 | 10 | 0 |
| 13 | 19 | 0 | | 2 Cuts W. Soda. | 1 | 10 | 0 |
| | 17 | 0 | 28th | ½ Cwt Copper | 1 | 12 | 6 |
| 2 | 16 | 0 | | ½ Cwt. W. Soda | 1 | 2 | 6 |
| 5 | 12 | 6 | Sept. 25th | 2 lb Tea. | | 11 | 6 |
| 1 | 9 | 0 | | 60 Players. | | 8 | 3 |
| 5 | 12 | 6 | | 6 lb Butter | 1 | 4 | 6 |
| | 14 | 6 | (Water) | 4½ lbs Biscuits | | 9 | 4 |
| | 14 | 2 | | 1 St Sugar | | 8 | 2 |
| 1 | 6 | 0 | | | £ 121 | 19 | 10 |
| | 12 | 3 | | | | | |
| 93 | 4 | 7 | | | | | |

A page in the ledger, dated 1958, gives an idea of the range of seasonal items that were ordered in the shop. In April grass seed was popular, also alsike and white clover was mixed with it. In May lime and potato manure were ordered. To counteract the potato blight in July, copper and washing soda was the mixture needed.

# BUILDING MATERIALS

At the hardware counter, in separate drawers, there was a whole range of nails - flooring nails, ceiling nails, wire nails, asbestos nails, slating nails, screw nails and ordinary nails of varying lengths. They were weighed on a weighbridge kept in the hardware department and then put into strong brown bags. There seemed to be a great need for nails in the farmyard.

Sometimes if the nails got mixed up we had a job separating them into their right compartments. Nobody liked that job as they were sharp to handle in quantities.

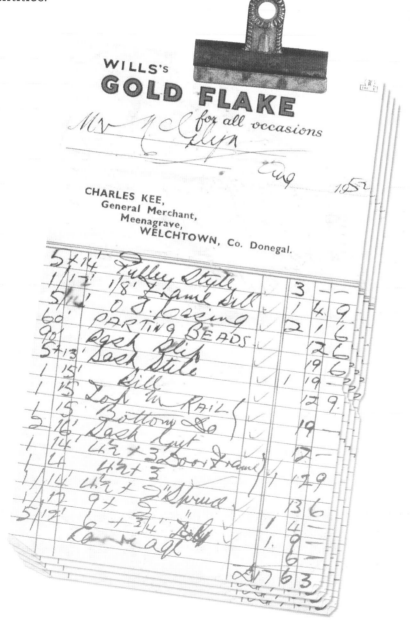

Timber was stored in a shed in the backyard. It came from timber merchants Herrons in Sligo. Large planks with the name burnt into the ends were ordered for all sorts of jobs.

Wire products were in great demand, such as barbed wire, netting wire and sheep wire.

The tradesmen that we knew were on the other side of the water, over in Corlecky. The other side was across the River Finn. Abbie and Tommy Patton were two brothers who had learned their trade from their father.

Abbie's father was John Patton, the Field Corlecky. He built the Kee house in the Orchard. The labour cost £18.

Paddy Patton, his brother, had a scutch mill, a saw-mill and a corn mill powered by a waterwheel. In the summer when trade in the mill was slack they built houses.

*Tommy, Albert and Abbie Patton*

Many houses were thatched. As time progressed it was getting harder to find the right thatch that would last for a number of years. Tin and asbestos had come on the market. Even today these roofs can still be seen in the countryside. Asbestos sheets were used during the war as tin was in short supply. Asbestos was heavy so stronger timbers were needed. It was also a brittle product that would crack easily. In very hot weather the asbestos would expand and this would cause problems when the rain came. After the war people wanted to use tin instead as it was more economical since lighter timbers could be used. If the tin was painted regularly with a good oxide paint it could last a long time. Later asbestos slates became popular. Nobody ever imagined that one day the asbestos would cause health problems and a licence would be needed for its removal.

When Abbie got a job he would come with his order to the shop. In 1964 he had a job putting a roof on Eddie Foy's house. The order was sent to Hanley's in Sligo. Within a week the load arrived and was redirected to the site. From the invoice it is interesting to see the material required and the amount of money it took to do the job.

**INVOICE**

# HANLEY & CO. LTD.

MERCHANTS AND BUILDERS' PROVIDERS

g. No. 8 Q 35373

O KEE ESQ
WELCHTOWN
CO DONEGAL

**OLD MARKET STREET**

AND

**LYNN'S DOCK**

**SLIGO**

| Date: 8/'64 | Invoice No. 143555 | Order No. | Per |
|---|---|---|---|

OURS TO E MOY, BALLYBOFEY

63/6' 22G GALV IRON @ 2/6.D FT PLUS 2½
1/18 - 4 X 3 @ 112/3D PER 100 FT LESS 8½%
3 X/2 - 21/15 @ 57/9D PER 100 FT LESS 8½%
7 X 1 - 2/15 1/12 @ 58/3D PER 100 FT LESS 8½%
3 X 2 - 21/15 @ 57/9D PER 100 FT LESS 8½%

SURCHARGE

CARRIAGE

| | | |
|---|---|---|
| 53 | 3 | 7 |
| | 13 | 5 |
| 3 | 13 | 3 |
| 1 | 6 | 0 |
| 18 | 6 | |
| 1 | 14 | 7 |
| 2 | – | – |

72 11 3
12 14 9
£71 2 10

76 5 10

CONDITIONS OF SALE PRINTED ON THE BACK

# OIL

The oil tank was also in the back yard opposite the barrel of rain water. That was handy when the paraffin oil was filled into the jars then you could wash your hands in the barrel. The quantities were small ½ pt or even ¼ pt. That was all it needed for a Tilley lamp or an oil lamp.

A note had to be kept of all oil that was sold.

Even after the introduction of electricity there were still a lot of homes using oil in lamps.

# DONEGAL OIL COMPANY

**DONEGAL OIL CO. LTD.**
PORT ROAD, LETTERKENNY
CO. DONEGAL

**INVOICE**

AD/11/61

Depot:
Railway Goods Yd.,
Killybegs

Phone Nos:
Killybegs          35
Letterkenny        14
(3 Lines)

Directors: J. C. Stewart F.C.A., R. T. McMahon,
A. E. McMahon (Managing), M. J. Geary (Sales Director)

**AUTHORISED DISTRIBUTORS FOR IRISH SHELL AND BP LIMITED**

764  Ledger

Supplied to :— *Mr Chas Kee*

*Meenagrave*
*Ballybofey*

A|c of

| | REP. | C.O.T. | P.CL. |
|---|---|---|---|
| | | 70 | |
| | COMM. | DUTY | T.TAX. |
| | | | |
| | | | M.O.D. |
| | | | 0 |

**D No 4775**

DATE *15-10-68*

VEHICLE No. *857*   ORDER No. *D*

The hydrocarbon oils and marked oils specified in this Section 1 of Invoice have been delivered free of customs/excise duty, or on rebate of such duty, and must not be used for combustion in the engine of a motor vehicle or kept in the fuel tank of such vehicle. Any person so doing, renders himself liable for proceedings with penalties.

| | Brand | Pkg. | | Galls./Lbs. | Price | £ | s. | d. |
|---|---|---|---|---|---|---|---|---|
| **1** | AGR. MRKT. | 34001 | SHELLSPARK | | | | | |
| | | 40504 | BP DIESOLITE (MARKED OIL) | 50 | 1/10½ | 4 | 13 | 9 |
| | DOM. MRKT. | 30101 | ALADDIN PINK | | | | | |
| | | 31003 | BP DOMESTICOL | | | | | |
| | | 40503 | SHELL DOMESTIC Fuel Oil (MARKED OIL) | | | | | |
| | IND. MRKT. | 40502 | SHELL GAS OIL C I (MARKED OIL) | | | | | |
| | | 40508 | SHELL GAS OIL S H (MARKED OIL) | | | | | 2 | 1 |
| | MARINE | 40501 | BP GASOLEUM (MARKED OIL) | | | | | |

| Brand Code | Pkg. Code | **LUBRICANTS** | Packages No. | Type |
|---|---|---|---|---|
| | | | | |

The Duty of Customs/Excise chargeable on Hydrocarbon Oil has been paid on the oil specified in this Section 2 of Invoice and no rebate of such duty has been allowed thereon.

| | DIESEL FUEL FOR ROAD VEHICLES | 17002 | BP DIESEL | | | | | |
|---|---|---|---|---|---|---|---|---|
| **2** | | 17001 | SHELL DIESOLINE | | | 4 | 11 | 8 |

| | | | | | SUB-TOTAL | 4 | 11 | 8 |
|---|---|---|---|---|---|---|---|---|
| | | | | | | | 2 | 5 |

TURNOVER TAX CHARGE (if applicable)

| RETURNABLE PACKAGES | D/d. | Retd. | Nett D/d. | Nett Retd. | @ |
|---|---|---|---|---|---|
| 90932  LIGHT STEEL BARRELS | | | | | |

| | | BALANCE | Debit | 4 | 14 | 1 |
|---|---|---|---|---|---|---|
| | | | Credit | | | |

E. & O. E.

Received Delivery subject to Conditions overleaf

Received Packages Returned

**TERMS NETT**
Received with thanks payment as above

CHEQUE
CASH

CUSTOMERS ARE REQUESTED TO READ THE CONDITIONS OF SALE PRINTED ON THE BACK

The oil came from the Donegal Oil Company based in Letterkenny. One of the directors was Mr. Michael Geary. He was the sales director.

Michael Geary

Marjorie with Mrs. Geary

Many years later I was fortunate to meet his daughter Marjorie, who worked in the Irish Room in Coleraine library. She kindly supplied me with a little booklet on the history of the Donegal Oil Company.

Marjorie Geary pictured outside the premises in Letterkenny

*Extract from a history of the Donegal Oil Company*

## DONEGAL OIL CO. LTD - 1954 - 1979.

### - A SHORT HISTORY -

The company came into being on July 5th 1954. Initially it was based in the old Shell Depot (no longer in existence) but within a year moved to its present location then a spanking new depot. The first directors were Arthur McMahon, his late brother Robert, J. C. Stewart and J. F. Heron both also deceased. Michael Geary resigned from Irish Shell to become the company's first and, to date its only Chief Executive. Jim Kennedy made a similar move as storekeeper. Drivers Jimmy Kelly and Fred Boyle both also sadly deceased, Pat Dunne, Charlie Moore, Jim Ponsonby, Eunan Blake (soon to achieve national eminence as a soccer footballer and later recognition as a widely respected Senior Football Manager), Michael Sweeney, Jimmy Mackey, John Doherty and James Meehan from Killybegs all made the switch from Shell to the new company. Kathleen Farren (now Mrs. Pat Harkin) joined as book-keeper and this staff of thirteen set about expanding and consolidating the fledgling organisation.

By following energetically, the managers strict competitive strategy, that of keen customer service, the sales drivers rapidly built up a sizeable agricultural market share. In the early years, however, poor quality, aging delivery trucks which at the outset had been taken over from Shell soon became liabilities. Management faced up to the problem by introducing a phased replacement programme which was completed in the mid sixties. By then the company had a relatively young delivery fleet and a rapidly expanding market boosted by the Oil Fired Heating upsurge. The depot, still only ten years old, was already too small to cope with the growth rate. In 1964 Shell began the depot extension programme which eventually quadrupled storage capacity and doubled the yard area. The soundness of that expansion plan is manifest to-day. Thus ended a significant phase in the company's development, one marked by able directive leadership, a hard working staff and attention to customer service culminating in attaining market leadership.

The next phase saw the organisation continue to grow larger, at a faster pace and thus become more complex to administer. The female clerical staff increased to match the growing

need for detailed accounting and reporting systems, and computerisation was introduced. To-day under the skille facilitation of Kathleen McFadden, the firm's Credit Controller, Bridget Scally, Hilda Patton, Dolores McNulty Marian Canning and Ann Stoddart cheerfully take care of processing of orders, accounting and statistical informati

New names too were added, both to the Board and staff, a "Anno Domini" took its toll of the older members. The company got a new chairman in Arthur's son Derek, now a internationally known businessman and motor racing patro Accountant Donal MacLochlainn replaced J. C. Stewart w died in 1972 and Michael Geary became Managing Directo In December 1979 Jim Kennedy became the newest additie to the Board.

Jim Harvey had long since taken over the one driver depo in Killybegs and proceeded to do a great job in coping with the huge volume increase in the marine and inland markets. Charlie Moore, Jimmy Kelly, Pat Dunne and Fr Boyle retired and new faces to appear and play major role in further building the company were Eddie Dunne (since left to launch his own successful business career), Leon Toye, Barney Harkin, Derek Wasson, Hugh McDaid, Hugh Mailey, Billy Gallagher, Ed. Moore, Sean Barrett, James Wilson, Eamonn Russell, David Cooke, and latterly Gabri Crawford and George Baskin. Seamus Gorman also joinec the organisation as salesman.

The market continued buoyant and stable. As the county became more industrialised and the marine industry expanded massively, oil distribution problems grew afresh. Solutions, however, were not long in forthcoming Delivery vehicles were again systematically replaced by even bigger trucks with larger carrying capacities and fitted with the most up-to-date equipment. The fleet also grew in number and now included necessary back-up vehicles. The expansion programme was aided by the introduction of articulated tractor trailer units with accompanying flexibility. The long term benefits of this strategy are in evidence to-day.

The stable growth period from the mid sixties was rudely interrupted in 1973 by the Middle-East war and subsequen oil price increases. The industry has never been the sar since.

# Half Days

Working hours in a country shop were long. Taking a half-day holiday during the week was normal practice. Wednesday was the half-day in our shop. It provided my father with time to do other things. Many Wednesday afternoons were spent in Ballybofey at the IAWS ordering items for the shop.

The Irish Agricultural Wholesale Society was set up in 1897. Initially it concentrated on seed and fertiliser but later expanded to flour, insecticides and many dry products. Entrance to the IAWS branch in Ballybofey was through a door in Navenney Street. Once inside it was a maze of shelving from the floor to ceiling. My father had a long list of items to order. We loved to have a look at the shoe section. Shoe boxes were piled high on the shelves. I remember getting a mustard pair of shoes for Sunday. They had a little heel and were beautiful.

On other days my father would collect us at school in Lifford and we would spend the afternoon in Strabane. He had always a business call to make. Woolworths in Strabane was always a great attraction for us. Known as the 3d and 6d. store it was a wonderful place to explore. To walk around the store and to be able to touch the products on display was a new concept in shopping. There were always bargains to be had.

*A typical Woolworth store*

He also went to Londonderry on occasions to Crockett and Guys. The well known Austins department store in the Diamond had wonderful shop window displays. It was a shop to visit only on very special occasions.

On the way home we were anxious about crossing the border. It had been established in 1921 and made trading with neighbouring counties very difficult. From Strabane we crossed the border at Lifford or if we were coming from Derry we crossed it at Monellan. We had to pass through two customs - one the Northern Ireland customs and a few hundred yards along the road was the Free State customs. Goods had to be declared.

No. 63 (Solo).

**GOODS REMOVED FROM PLACES IN THE STATE THROUGH NORTHERN IRELAND TO OTHER PLACES IN THE STATE.**

Exit:

Serial No.

Station Date Stamp

Station of Exit

Officer

Station of Re-entry

Number of Wagon, etc. in which goods will re-enter the State.

(To be completed by the Railway Company)

Re-entry:—

Rotation No.

Station Date Stamp

To the Export Officer of Customs and Excise at

The undermentioned goods are produced herewith for removal through Northern Ireland to the address shown below.

Officer.

| Marks and Numbers of Packages | Number of Packages | Name and Address of Consignee | GOODS | |
|---|---|---|---|---|
| | | | Description | Weight or Quantity |
| | | | | |

Total number of Packages (in words at length)

Signature of Consignor or his authorised Representative

Name of Consignee(s)

Place of Business

Date

**Certificate of Officer of Customs and Excise (Northern Ireland).**

I certify that the above-mentioned Goods arrived at in Northern Ireland, with the Irish Customs seals intact, that they were transhipped without alteration or abstraction of any of the packages or the addition of any packages or goods, and that the British Customs seals numbers were affixed at the conclusion of the transhipment.

Officer of Customs and Excise.

Station Date Stamp

This certificate is only required where goods are transhipped in course of removal

G O ————— 3S and "Instructions to Assistant Preventive Officers" Par. 49
1948

Sec. 667/3606/50

Dublin: Printed under the authority of the Stationery Office, and to be purchased from the Government Publications Sale Office, G.P.O. Arcade, Dublin, or through any bookseller.

Price 2d. each. Per 100 4/-.

X39227.31373.12/53.500,000.W.&S.M.(I.)Ltd. Est. 680A

Smuggling was an activity that most people indulged in. It was not seen as a crime by the population. The authorities thought differently.

The customs officers always looked very stern. My father would always be polite and we were warned to keep quiet in the back seat. We were scared that items we had purchased in the north would be taken off us. Sometimes we had to wear the items of clothing that we purchased over our own clothes or we hid them under our seats. How we dreaded the occasions when we were asked to get out of the car while they searched the vehicle.

Worse still was the outbreak of Foot and Mouth disease in 1967 when we had to disembark and wipe our feet on a disinfectant mat.

*The Customs Post at Lifford*

The best half-days were in the summer when we went to the seaside. The Sunday School excursion was on the first Wednesday in June. We never went in the bus but took our own car. The sight of the sea had us jumping up and down with joy. It was straight into the sea for our first dip of the year and afterwards we tucked into a picnic on the sand. I can never remember wet days in Rossnowlagh.

*Old Postcards of Rossnowlagh*

We had 6d. to spend in the little shop. It was an Aladdin's cave for eager customers. Rock was the usual purchase. It kept us chewing the whole way home.

*Charlie with his daughters Pearl and Dorothy at Rossnowlagh*

Barnes' Gap, Co. Donegal.

In earlier times, when the train was running, we always started for home before it left. Our aim was to get to Barnesmore Gap in time to see it coming. What a sight to see the Wee Donegal pass through the gap with sometimes 11 coaches on the train. We would wave at the many children who were hanging out the carriage windows. Then it was a race for us to see if we could beat the train. "Faster, faster," we would shout to our father, "put the foot to the board." We would always win.

The Stranorlar - Donegal line was opened in 1882 and later it was expanded to Killybegs and Ballyshannon. Lord Lifford and his son-in-law Sir Samuel Hayes were instrumental in bringing the Finn Valley Railway to Co. Donegal.

RAILWAY BRIDGE.
BALLYBOFEY.

Leaving Stranorlar the line crossed the River Finn and climbed towards Meenglass halt. It passed Lough Mourne to the summit at Derg bridge halt that was 592 feet above sea level. Next stop was Barnesmore then on to Donegal through Lough Eske and Clar Bridge. There would be four more stops before Rossnowlagh - Drumbar, Laghey, Bridgetown and Ballintra. Excursion trains were popular right up until the line closed in 1959.

A trip to Bundoran was another favourite. The donkey rides on the beach were the big attraction.

*Charles senior and Charles junior on Bundoran beach*

Days out were the only holidays that most people got. Foreign holidays were for future generations. The only holidays my father took were Bank holidays. The shop would be closed on Saturday night and would re-open on Tuesday.

# CHRISTMAS

With the advent of Christmas, my sister put fairy lights in the shop window. We strung decorations made from crepe paper across the ceiling of the shop and added some holly to the shelves. Brown paper was in great demand as presents were posted to relatives in England. Sticks of wax were needed to seal the parcel.

Christmas boxes were expected from the shopkeeper. Calendars were ordered and eagerly awaited by customers. People who perhaps dealt very little in the shop all year would arrive at Christmas demanding a calendar.

1960
Calenders
for 1960

Calenders for 1960 (Calenders)

John Patton (Welchtown)
　Mrs M°Ginty
　George Blackburn
　John Blackburn
Tom (Sargan) Kee (Meenagrawer)
Tom Martin
Sarah Temple
W^m James Kee (Hill)
W^m Kee (Roundknows)
J Griffeth (Altnaguinea)
Woodside
Jim Kee (Mill)
Elias Griffeth
M° Kenna
B Scanlon
P Scanlon (Comon)
　Charlie Tom
Paky Welchtown
W^m Patton
Robert Kee
Saunders ☞ got two calenders
Billys Lizzie
Anne Patton
John Donnes (Paddy)
James M°Ginty
　Kee
Mary Roundknownes
Jim Lepper
Tom M°Cready
John M°Clean (Callen)
Mrs Smyth (Magheacorn)
Martha M°Clean

*My sister kept a note of who got calendars in 1960.*

| | | | |
|---|---|---|---|
| 1960 | n̄ D̄ | Jimmy Kee (to get) England | Oct 1960 56 |
| Calenders for 1960 | E R | Ruby Kee England (to get) | Calenders 8 for 1960 |
| | S | W<sup>m</sup> Kee (police) | 1958 |

England

| | |
|---|---|
| 1960 D | Jimmy Kee (to get) |
| Calenders E | Ruby Kee (to get) |
| for 1960 R | W<sup>m</sup> Kee (police) |
| S | Donald M<sup>c</sup>Ginty |
| 1 | Cecil Mahon |
| 9 | J. Boice (Lorain) |
| 6 | Mrs M<sup>c</sup>Clure |
| 0 | Dan M<sup>c</sup>Menamin |

Dennis M<sup>c</sup>Menamin

Mary Ann M<sup>c</sup>Cready

Jim M<sup>c</sup>glyn       Calenders for 1960

Pat M<sup>c</sup>cone

John Gallaher (Meenban)

Mrs Thompson (Welchtown)

Mrs younge (the gates)

Dan M<sup>c</sup>Glincey

H. bonner bonner (postman)

G. Rustard

M<sup>c</sup> Gilloway

J. M<sup>c</sup>Ginty

John Martin

John Brown

Tom Patton

Lizzie Jane

Charles Doherty Doherty

Paddy Roan

John Melly

Sarny Logue

Mrs J. M<sup>c</sup> Menamin

Pat Brown

~~Jack Patton~~

Etta Patton

Jim Hume

Paddy Moi

## Presents for customers

When a good customer arrived we were given the nod by my father. We were sent to the good room in the house with tissue paper to wrap either a barn brack or a cake. It was then brought through to the shop and discreetly placed in the customer's bag or basket. No words were spoken about it as there may have been other customers in the shop who didn't merit these gifts. A calendar was enough for them.

*100 calendars cost £10 2s 6d in 1964.*

*This was the verse inside one of the Christmas cards.*

This Christmas wish I send away,
With kindest thoughts
to you to-day
And hope that all its hours
will bless
Your future days with happiness.

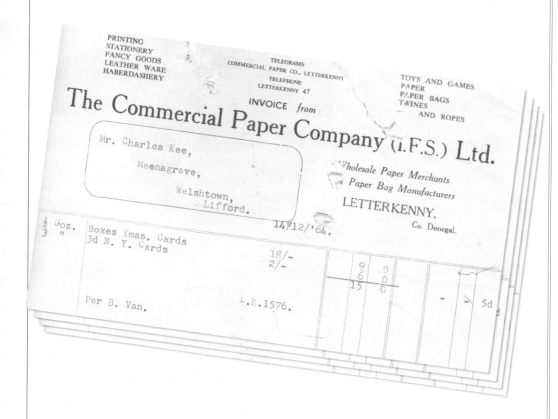

## Mummers in the shop

Every Christmas the mummers would roam the countryside going from house to house. They were known as Christmas Rhymers in other parts of the country. The shop door would burst open and in would come the actors. They were usually a motley crew. Sometimes the acting left a lot to be desired. Other times, if they had learned their lines well, it was fun. We all knew the rhymes. It was hard to recognise the young lads as they were in disguise. Girls never took part in this activity.

The sham fight on the floor was always a violent affair. It usually frightened us as we never knew whether it was for real or not. I liked the doctor the best with his bag and his ability to raise the dead. We always knew when wee Johnny Funny appeared what we had to do. "Go to the till and bring out a shilling," my father would say. If the performance was poor a sixpence would do. Sadly this custom died out in the mid 1960's. Thankfully it is now being revived in some parts of the country.

# Santa's visit

Santa Claus never forgot the children of the shop. A letter was written around the beginning of December and left on the mantelpiece in our parents' bedroom. A fire was always lit in this room in the winter as there was no central heating in the house.

It was amazing how the letters were able to float up the chimney and fly all the way to Lapland. We hung our stocking above the range in the kitchen. There was great talk at school about Santa. Did he or did he not exist? We believed because we discovered that if you didn't believe you got no presents! Among my father's receipts was an interesting invoice from 1964.

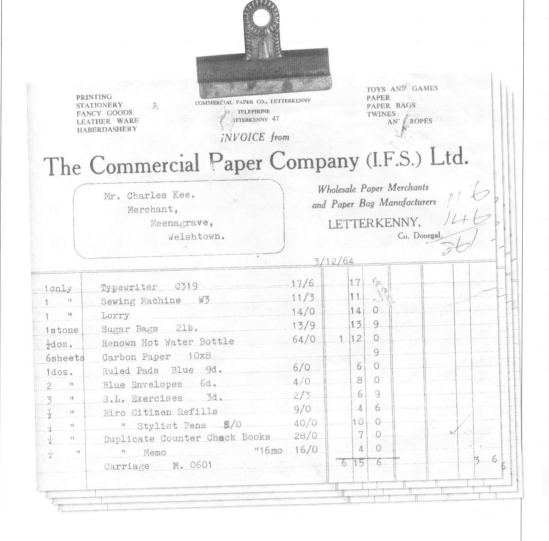

PRINTING
STATIONERY
FANCY GOODS
LEATHER WARE
HABERDASHERY

COMMERCIAL PAPER CO., LETTERKENNY
TELEPHONE
LETTERKENNY 47

*INVOICE from*

TOYS AND GAMES
PAPER
PAPER BAGS
TWINES
AND ROPES

## The Commercial Paper Company (I.F.S.) Ltd.

Mr. Charles Kee.
Merchant,
Meenagrave,
Welshtown.

*Wholesale Paper Merchants
and Paper Bag Manufacturers*

LETTERKENNY,
Co. Donegal,

3/12/64

| | | | | | |
|---|---|---|---|---|---|
| 1 only | Typewriter   C319 | 17/6 | 17 | 6 | |
| 1 " | Sewing Machine   W3 | 11/3 | 11 | 3 | |
| 1 " | Lorry | 14/0 | 14 | 0 | |
| 1 stone | Sugar Bags   2lb. | 13/9 | 13 | 9 | |
| ½doz. | Renown Hot Water Bottle | 64/0 | 1 12 | 0 | |
| 6 sheets | Carbon Paper   10x8 | | | 9 | |
| 1 doz. | Ruled Pads  Blue  9d. | 6/0 | 6 | 0 | |
| 2 " | Blue Envelopes   6d. | 4/0 | 8 | 0 | |
| 3 " | 3.L. Exercises   3d. | 2/3 | 6 | 9 | |
| ½ " | Biro Citizen Refills | 9/0 | 4 | 6 | |
| ½ " |  "  Stylist Pens  5/0 | 40/0 | 10 | 0 | |
| ½ " | Duplicate Counter Check Books | 28/0 | 7 | 0 | |
| ½ " |  "  Memo  "16mo | 16/0 | 4 | 0 | |
| | Carriage   M. 0601 | | 6 15 | 6 | 3  6 |

The first three items were our Christmas presents in 1964.

The typewriter was 17s 6d, the lorry was 14s 0d, and the sewing machine was 11s 3d. The typewriter was for my sister and the lorry for my brother. The sewing machine was for me. I can still remember the excitement of tearing open the box to discover a beautiful miniature sewing machine that I could use. I wanted to sew just like my mother.

One visitor who always brought us books at Christmas was the minister from my mother's home church. Being someone of importance he had to be entertained in the good room. It was usually chilly and sometimes smoky as the fire didn't draw too well. The dining-room table was set with the fine china that had belonged to Uncle Tom. We were well warned to be on our best behaviour. My sister took a fit of the giggles in the long silences as the minister was a man of a few words. It started the rest of us laughing too. My parents were mortified and we were punished accordingly after he left. However, we loved the books he brought us and treasure some of them to this day.

Christmas Day was simple. The food was mainly home produced. A goose was fattened for the occasion. Sometimes turkeys would be reared. None of these were sold in the shop. Currants and raisins, cherries and peel were more the items that were bought. Christmas cakes and plum puddings were made in most households. We spent Christmas Day at home enjoying our presents. There was little fuss.

*Susan Thompson with her children*
*Mary and Ernest in 1961*

# SUNDAYS

Saturday nights in the shop were social occasions. Men would gather from 8pm to do their shopping and then the storytelling would begin. By 10.30pm my father would be anxious to get the shop closed. If Packie was in full flight he hadn't a chance. Packie loved to tell stories, especially about horses.

Preparation for Sunday began on Saturday night. All the shoes in the house had to be polished. Potatoes were washed and vegetables prepared. If chicken was on the menu for Sunday dinner then my mother had to pull the neck of one of our hens in the backyard. I loved the job of plucking the feathers. Singeing the hairs with a flame was a tricky enough business. Methylated spirits was poured into a small container, usually an upturned lid, and then lit. You felt very grown up if you were allowed to do this task.

Bath time was next. It was in a tin bath in the kitchen. I often wonder how we managed. Next came our Sunday lessons rhymed off for as long as it took to know them word perfect. No excuses were taken.

Sunday clothes were aired as they hadn't been used all week. On Sunday morning the door of the shop remained firmly closed. There was an unwritten rule that no trading was carried out on a Sunday. Sunday was a day of rest.

*Shop closed on Sunday morning*

Church was always the place to go on Sunday morning. The bell would be rung to call worshippers and could be heard over a wide area. There would be a steady stream of people on the road dressed in their Sunday best. People walking, others on bicycles. Not many cars were in sight.

Church was a solemn occasion where children had to sit and were warned not to move. The more affluent you were the nearer to the front you sat. I remember costumes and furs that had seen many years wear. Hats came in all shapes and sizes. It was unthinkable that the day would come when hats would no longer be worn. Sometimes the smell of mothballs hung in the air. Our seat was half way up the church. On the other side of the church you could look out on the woods of Glenmore. It was easy to daydream. During the prayers you could sneak a peep at someone in the back of the congregation who took your fancy. If you were caught you were in trouble after church.

*Sunday School class outside Paradise House circa 1910*

*Mrs. Elizabeth Kee is seated. Leaning against her on the left is Tommy John Kee Millbrook. The little girl to the right is Lily Patton, Meenagrave (later McGonigle). The girl to the far right is Emma Kee, Meenagrave (later McCreery). Annie Patton is second from right. The boy to the far left is Andy Patton, Meenagrave. The boy standing at the back, behind the two little girls, is Charles Fooks. The lady behind Mrs. Kee at the back is Mrs. Guy Ferguson.*

Tom and his wife were deeply religious. They built a gospel hall at the back of the shop. Here they held meetings and invited speakers to conduct gospel meetings. It was well finished in the inside with wooden panelling. Pews were provided and even an organ was supplied. As the outside was corrugated iron, the pranksters had great fun throwing stones at the roof. The noise was deafening to those gathered inside. On one occasion a young lad threw a horse-shoe through the window narrowly missing someone who had stayed behind to pray. Later in my father's time, the hall was a great place for us to ride our bicycles on a wet day.

The Sunday school met on a Sunday afternoon and was attended by a large group of children. Eagerly awaited was the Christmas party. It was the highlight of the year. Egg boxes were arranged round the shop floor for seating. Games were played and each child got a bag of sweets or chocolate as a present. That was a real treat.

*St. John's Church revisited on 28th. April 2012 by Charles, Dorothy and Pearl*

The Clergy in the parish can be traced back to 1773. They came from different parts of the country. They were educated men and were treated with great respect. They were aloof from their congregation and their word was law. No one dared to call them by their Christian name.

Canon Arthur McQuade came in 1888. He baptised my father on the 9th. November 1913.

Other clergy were Cecil Homan, Josiah Haddock, Robert Devlin and Robert Henry Egar. There was a farm attached to the rectory which brought in extra income. Rev. Egar employed Frank Thomson to work on the farm and Mary Patton as a servant girl. Abbie Patton remembers that Rev. Josiah Haddock brought electricity to the rectory years before it came to the district. He built himself a generator with batteries and installed electricity in the rectory. Later he took it to the church. His parishioners were amazed at what he could do.

Rev. Fennell was the curate in charge from 1948 to 1954. He baptised the three of us. He later became head of R.E. at Annadale Grammar School, Belfast, and was education organiser for N.I. for 10 years until 1981.

Rev. Gerald Carson came to Kilteevogue with his mother in 1954 and stayed until 1957. Later in life he became an accomplished artist. He visited our shop often. He was the last clergyman to live in the rectory at Glenmore as the parish was amalgamated with Stranorlar and Meenglass in 1957.

Rev. Bertram came from Co. Cavan. He was in Kilteevogue from 1958-1965. I remember being prepared for confirmation in his time. The classes were in the rectory and ran for a number of weeks. We were fearful of the examination but it didn't prove too difficult. I can't remember anyone who failed.

*Confirmation pictures*

*Canon Moore, Mrs Moore, Teech Kee and Jimmy Kee*

Rev. Noel Moore was there when we left in 1968. He was born in Newbliss, Co. Monaghan and became a canon in St. Columb's Cathedral, Londonderry, in 1989.

When the church service was over we were like wild birds released from a cage. First stop was the spout at the gatehouse to Glenmore. The water was refreshing even though we once found a dead sheep in the stream further up the woods. Then it was home for a lovely dinner. Lamb was our favourite roast.

When our Sunday clothes were changed we went for a walk with our father. It was the only day that we had him to ourselves. Our favourite walk was across the old road and up the hills to the High Brae. From there you could see in all directions. The wind was always strong in our faces. When we got to the top it was time to rest. My father would point out landmarks in the distance. There was the Gorey Hill, where once the Styles had tried to mine silver. They brought miners from England in 1775 but no silver was found. The ore was transported on the horses' backs. We loved to hear about the tunnel they dug. It was about 30 yards long and was 6 feet high. It sounded like a good place to explore. We were warned not to go near it.

Further to the west was the Three Tops. We were familiar with them, as we would often deliver meal up the Corlecky road that lead to the top. Nowadays there is a large wind farm seen for miles around. The mountain to the west rising to 1199 feet was called Altnapaste. We were still too young to climb it.

Soon it was time to move on. There were ditches to climb and sometimes barbed wire to negotiate. My father was gentle with us as we struggled to keep up. As little legs grew tired we always wanted a piggy back. It wasn't easy with three small children on tow.

My father loved to call on people when he was out for a walk. There were people we liked to call on and others we were not so keen on. We would sit out on the bank at these houses and wait for him.

One house we loved him to call on was further over the hill. The cottage was across a stream and a mother and daughter lived there. It was spotlessly clean and everything was painted blue in the kitchen. The dresser was blue, the table legs were blue the chairs were blue. The mother hadn't been well and was in bed. "Come down to the room," Lizzie said. It was the good room where visitors were taken. There was no fire lit that day. She pulled back a lace curtain and there, in a high bed tucked in an outshot off the room, was her mother. It looked so cosy and warm.

If we were energetic we would follow the river to the footbridge and head towards Cloghan. We loved to stand on the Ivy Bridge and see the waters swirling far below. Occasionally we would see the salmon leap in the water. It was a wonderful sight.

We didn't know that this was a very famous part of the River Finn. Anglers from England and further afield could read about it in angling magazines and many would come to fish there.

*The Birthplace of Isaac Butts*

My father would point out where Isaac Butts was born. We didn't know how important a man he was. Later in school we learned of his role in Home Rule and tenants right. The Glebe house where he lived had been built by his father Rev. Butts in 1779.

Beyond his house were the ruins of a church. This church was originally erected by a virgin named Teevogue Nee Divenney. It was rebuilt in 1774 and had seating for 250 people.

For generations our family had worshipped there until the new church was built at Glenmore.

*The Kee sisters with Charlie McCreery*

On the way home we met others out for a walk. We always stopped for a chat. There was fun and laughter as we exchanged pleasantries.

If Sunday was wet we had to entertain ourselves indoors. We usually played the piano or read books. Sometimes, if we had company, we played church on the stairs. We pretended that it was the gallery. My sister did the preaching. I played the piano and my brother lifted the collection. If my sister was going on a bit we told her to "close up". You couldn't say that to the clergyman in church.

*A group of cousins with my mother Jennie*

Most Sundays evenings we went to visit our grandparents. As my mother was one of nine children there were plenty of cousins around to play with out on the street. That's where children were sent so the adults could talk in the kitchen. Before we left home we would go into the shop and fill a bag of sweets for our granny. She liked mint sweets best.

She would be sitting in an armchair and we took it in turns to give her the little bag. She didn't hug or kiss us but she would shake our hand. That meant a lot.

All too soon the day of rest was over.

*My Grandparents - Samuel and Mary Matilda McClean*

# CONCLUSION

Memories come flooding back as I once again travel along the road that led to my father's shop.

Passing the wood and the entrance to Glenmore Castle it is hard to imagine a once busy place where carriages swept up the avenue to visit the Styles family. The rhododendrons lined both sides of the avenue and were magnificent in full bloom.

Across the river I can make out a few familiar landmarks among the many new houses that dot the hillside. Highview was built by a man who had been to America. It was where Glenmore Castle was originally going to be sited.

It is almost impossible now to see the forge. We passed it every day on our way to school. The blacksmith was Jim Leeper. There were always horses to be shod. The horseshoes were ordered in our shop. They came in different sizes.

I can see Welshtown School. The excitement for us the day that school was opened knew no bounds. The old school had served the population well. It was the only education that the older generations got. However, it was adequate for most of the population.

*Welshtown New School opened in 1962*

Welshtown had a cluster of houses but it was never called a village. The public house and post office are no more.

Many of the old faces are gone. Annie Young lived in the railway gate house by the church. All those steps that she ran down to close the gates for the passing train have disappeared.

*The Railway Gatehouse*

It was always good to stop at the spout for a sup of water at McKenna's. Opposite was the gate that we used which led to St. John's church. It has disappeared. I recently found a drawing of the gate in the Public Record office in Belfast. It had been planned with great detail.

*The Gatehouse at Glenmore*

A little further along is a two-storied house on the side of the road. It looks just the same as it has always done. Sometimes the curtain would move as we passed on our bicycles. We never dallied there. It was best to pedal furiously to reach the top of the hill. We could stop there for a breather.

I never tire of the view from John's brae. I imagine that John was one of the Kees who lived up the lane in the Woodside - an ancestor of my own.

There is a good view of the River Finn. Sadly the island is no more. It was our playground and where we watched the otters slide in and out of the water. Water dogs we called them.

Here and there, just visible, are the remains of the railway. What a wonderful attraction that would have made for the modern tourists on their way to Glenties and the wild Atlantic way.

*View from John's Brae towards the shop*

Altnapaste looks as magnificient as ever. It was hard to climb but worth the effort. Our nearest neighbours were the Pattons. They were our constant companions in all sorts of fun and adventures. In the centre of the picture the gable end of the shop is visible. It is hard to believe we once played tennis with our neighbours in front of the shop. We had only to stop occasionally to allow a vehicle to pass. I can remember the crowds of people who walked on this road. Today there is no one in sight.

Forty-six years have passed since my father sold the shop in Meenagrave. Over the years the new owner, Mrs. Ann McGlynn, made alterations to suit the changing times. The wooden counters are long gone and customers now serve themselves. The post office from Welshtown has been added.

It is my hope that this country shop will continue to trade for many more generations

# CUSTOMERS IN THE SHOP

in the 1950s and 60s
taken from the ledgers

Patrick Brown
Jim Brown
Ronnie Barclay, Killtyfergal
Andy Blackburn, Corlecky
Hugh Bonner, postman
Joe Bonner, blacksmith
John Blackburn, Corlecky
Sam Blackburn
F. Boyle Reelin
John Bonner
Jim Bonner, Teenybanns
John Boyce
John Bustard
George Bustard
Kate Blackburn
John Bonner
Bob Blackburn
George Blackburn
Andy Baskin
Pat Breslin
Dick Armstrong
Jim Bell
Victor Bell
Tony Carlin
Paddy Carlin
Rev. Carson
Mrs J Campbell
Mosey Chambers
Billy Chambers
Alex Chambers, Corlecky
William Chambers,
Meenagrave
Paddy Campbell
Master Campbell,
Brockagh
Hugh Campbell
County Council
John Coyle, Reelin
James Coyle, Ballykerrigan
Dr. & Mrs. Crawford
Arthur Donaldson
Thomas Doherty

Harry Daisley
Charles Doherty
Peter Doherty
Mick Doherty
Paddy Doherty
A. Dennison
Joe Ferguson
C. Gallagher
John Gallagher
Sally Gallagher
Eddie Gibbons, PO
Frank Given
Elias Griffith
John Griffith
Frank Harkin
John Harkin, smith
Joe Harkin, smith
Madge Hone
A. Houston
Mrs Kee PO
Mrs. C. Kee, Welchtown
Wm. Kee, policeman
Wm. James Kee
Tommy Kee, Sergeant
Matt Kee, Roundnows
William Kee, Roundnows
Matt Kee, Highview
Albert Kee
Betty Kee
Jamie Kelly
John Kelly
Paddy Logue
Dan Lafferty
John McClean
Sammy McClean
Chas. McCready
Paddy McDermott
Conal McGinty
Peter McGinty
Pat McGinley
Eddie McGlynn
Peter McGlynn

James McGonigle
Sam McMenamim
Denis McMenamim
Chas. McNamee
Bridig McNamee
Master Magee
Jim Magee, Ballynatone
John Martin
Tommy Martin
Cecil Mahon
Hugh Mooney
Patsy Molloy
Paddy Patton
Abbey patton
John Patton
Jack Patton
Wm. Patton
John Quinn
Anna Bella Quinn
Paddy Roan
John Roulston
Martha Roulston
Joe Scanlon
Ernie Thompson,
Welshtown
Wm. Thompson, Gorey
Jamie Temple

# List of Suppliers

## Donegal

### Charles Kelly Ltd.
Letterkenny Mills
Ramelton Mills
*Grain millers*
*Flour factors*
*Timber importers*

### Grant Bros Ltd.
Buncrana
High toast snuff and tobacco manufacturers
Wholesale cigarette merchants

### William Thompson & Co.
Letterkenny
*Importers of manure, cement, feeding stuffs, implement agents, seed merchants*

### Robert Smyth & Sons
Swilly Valley Mills, Ballindrait, Lifford
Canal Basin Mills, Strabane

### McConnell & Co. (Donegal) Ltd.
Bridgend
*Wholesale grocers, druggists and tea merchants*

### John Mortimer & Co.
Bridgend
Lifford
*Wholesale Druggist and General Merchant*

### Thomas Cassidy & Co.
Eske Stores
Donegal
*Wholesale paper and twine merchants*

## The Commercial Paper Co. Ltd.
Letterkenny
*Wholesale paper merchants*
*Paper bag manufacturers*

## Wm. McKinney and Sons Ltd.
Letterkenny
Oatfield Confectionary Works

## James McColgan & Co. Ltd.
Buncrana
*General hardware, ironmongery, builders providers and electrical factors*

## Irish Agricultural Wholesale Society Ltd.
Ballybofey

## Henry McNulty
Ballybofey
*Wholesale Grocer, confectioner and tobacconist*

## A. Magee & Sons Ltd.
Cappry
Ballybofey
*Potato & Fertiliser Merchants*

## William Doherty & Sons
Convoy
*Printers and Wholesale Merchants*

## Donegal Oil Company Ltd.
Port Rd
Letterkenny

## WH Raitt & Son
Stranorlar
*Builders providers, hardware merchants, fuel suppliers, licensed firearm dealers, general grocers, Kosangas dealers, sports goods, china & glassware*

## Peter McGinty
Main St
Donegal
*Wholesale fruit and general merchant*

## Samuel Wilson
Meetinghouse St
Raphoe
*Butter merchant*

## J. Hannigan & Sons
Stranorlar
*Bacon, cooked ham and sausage wholesalers*

## Donegal Bacon Company Ltd.
Letterkenny

## Dunlevy & Company
The Diamond
Donegal
*Hardware, ironmongery, hollow-ware, ranges, grates and cookers
Lighting, heating, electrical, sanitary, china, glass and earthenware,
haberdashery, medical sundries, stationery, paper and printing, fancy,
souvenir and religious goods, floor covering, wallpapers and paints*

## James Doherty
Main St
Letterkenny
*Purveyor of high-class meat*

## James White & Co.
The Mall
Ballyshannon
*Vivo wholesalers*

## Joseph Kelly
Frosses
*Wholesale Fruit Merchant*

## McGowan Bros Ltd.
Ballybofey
*Fruit Importers & Distributors*

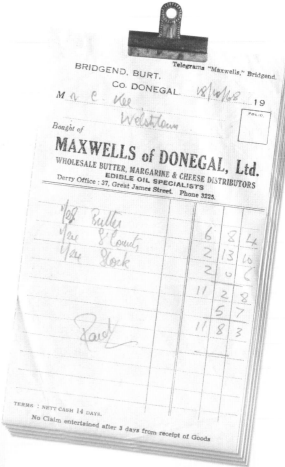

# SLIGO

## R. & R. Gorman
Adelaide St
Sligo
*Grain, flour and hardware merchants*

## Blackwood & Co.
5, 6, & 7 Grattan St
Sligo
*Wholesale grocers, tea importers and provision merchants*

## W.A. & A.F. Woods Ltd.
Castle St
Sligo
*Wholesale merchants and factors*

## Heron and Sons
44 High St
Sligo
*Direct importers and distributors*

## D.M. Hanley & Co. Ltd.
Old Market St
& Lynn's Dock
Sligo
*Timber merchants and builders providers*

# DUBLIN

## Beechams of Ireland
Long Mile Rd
Drimnagh
Dublin

## W.D. & H.O. Wills and Wm. Clarke & Sons
Branch of Players and Wills (Ireland) Ltd.
South Circular Rd
Dublin 8

## McCarroll Group Distributors Ltd.
Grand parade
Dublin

## H. & E. Musgrave (Dublin) Ltd.
45 Marrowbone Lane
Dublin 8
*Nambarrie and Namosa tea*

## W. & R. Jacob & Co., Ltd.
Dublin 8
*Biscuit Manufacturers*

## Baker Wardell & Co. Ltd.
76 & 82 Thomas St
Dublin 8
*Wholesale Tea Sugar and Coffee Merchants*

## Gallagher (Dublin) Ltd.
68 Upper Stephen St
Dublin 8
*Tobacco Manufacturers*

## Lamb Bros (Dublin) Ltd.
Naas Rd
Dublin 12
*Fruit preservers*

## W. & M. Taylor Ltd.
Dublin 8
*Tobacco & snuff manufacturers.*

# DERRY

## Crockett & Guy
Strand Rd
Londonderry
*Ironmongers and hardware merchants*

# LIMERICK

## Ranks
Dock Road
Limerick
*Blue cross and animal foods*

## Claremorris
McCallig Bros
*Wholesale fancy goods importers*
*China and hardware merchants*

Telephone 3670   STATEMENT

**MARKET YARD,**
**SLIGO**   ...21/10/08......   19......

Mrs...... *b tree*

...... *Meenagrane* ......

# STUART & PORTER
### WHOLESALE HARDWARE MERCHANTS

| | | | | Debit | | | Credit | | Balance | |
|---|---|---|---|---|---|---|---|---|---|---|
| Sept | 5 | 5/8 | 11 | 14 | 9 | | | £ | 11 | 14 | 9 |
| | | | | | | D Wc | | 5 | 9 |
| | | | | | | | 11 | 9 | 0 |
| | | | | | acc Bucket | | 2 | 6 |
| | | | | | | £ | 11 · 6 · 6 |

Nº   837   **MARKET YARD, SLIGO**

21 = 10 = 1968

Received from *Mr. b. Kee*

*Meenagrane*

the sum of *Eleven* ......Pounds

...... *Six* ......Shillings and ...... *Six* ......Pence

For   **STUART & PORTER**

£   11 : 6 : 6   With Thanks
8 : 3   Per *J Stuart*

## About the Author

Pearl Hutchinson has been involved in local history for over 30 years. She is chairperson of Kilrea Local History Group and has been instrumental in recording and publishing six books on the history of Kilrea in Co. Derry.

She is vice chairman of the Coleraine branch of the North of Ireland Family History Society and has a keen interest in helping people trace their family trees.

Pearl was born in the townland of Meenagrave in Co. Donegal where her father owned a country shop. Her love of storytelling grew from helping to attend customers in the shop.

She is an active member of Causeway Yarnspinners and through her reminiscence work she likes to encourage other people to tell their stories.

She hopes that this story will bring back nostalgic memories of a time when the shopkeeper stood behind the wooden counter ready to serve the customer.

*Today, in 2014, the shop in Meenagrave is still in existence.*
*It now incorporates Welchtown Post Office*
*and is owned by Mr. and Mrs. Francie McGlynn.*